Simply comfort

feel-good favorites for your slow cooker & air fryer

Fish & Chips, page 298

also by lisa lillien

HUNGRY GIRL:
Recipes and Survival Strategies for Guilt-Free Eating in the Real World

HUNGRY GIRL 200 UNDER 200:
200 Recipes Under 200 Calories

HUNGRY GIRL 1-2-3:
The Easiest, Most Delicious, Guilt-Free Recipes on the Planet

HUNGRY GIRL HAPPY HOUR:
75 Recipes for Amazingly Fantastic Guilt-Free Cocktails & Party Foods

HUNGRY GIRL 300 UNDER 300:
300 Breakfast, Lunch & Dinner Dishes Under 300 Calories

HUNGRY GIRL SUPERMARKET SURVIVAL:
Aisle by Aisle, HG-Style!

HUNGRY GIRL TO THE MAX!
The Ultimate Guilt-Free Cookbook

HUNGRY GIRL 200 UNDER 200 JUST DESSERTS:
200 Recipes Under 200 Calories

THE HUNGRY GIRL DIET

THE HUNGRY GIRL DIET COOKBOOK:
Healthy Recipes for Mix-n-Match Meals & Snacks

HUNGRY GIRL CLEAN & HUNGRY:
Easy All-Natural Recipes for Healthy Eating in the Real World

HUNGRY GIRL CLEAN & HUNGRY OBSESSED!
All-Natural Recipes for the Foods You Can't Live Without

HUNGRY GIRL SIMPLY 6:
All-Natural Recipes with 6 Ingredients or Less

HUNGRY GIRL FAST & EASY:
All-Natural Recipes in 30 Minutes or Less

HUNGRY GIRL: THE OFFICIAL SURVIVAL GUIDES:
Tips & Tricks for Guilt-Free Eating
(audio book)

HUNGRY GIRL CHEW THE RIGHT THING:
Supreme Makeovers for 50 Foods You Crave
(recipe cards)

Hungry Girl

Simply comfort

feel-good favorites for your slow cooker & air fryer

#1 *New York Times* Bestselling Author

Lisa Lillien

St. Martin's Griffin

New York

Tuscan Steak Stew,
page 57

get more
Hungry Girl

For the latest better-for-you recipes, food finds, healthy-eating tips & tricks, and MORE . . .

✉ **Subscribe for FREE daily emails** at hungry-girl.com

f **Follow Lisa on Facebook** at facebook.com/hungrygirl

👥 **Join the Hungry Girl Community: What's Chewin'? group** on Facebook

📷 **Follow Lisa on Instagram** . . . She's @hungrygirl

🎧 **Listen to the *Hungry Girl: Chew the Right Thing!* podcast** at hungry-girl.com/podcast

📌 **Follow Hungry Girl on Pinterest** at pinterest.com/hungrygirl

The author's references to various brand-name products and services are for informational purposes only and are not intended to suggest endorsement or sponsorship of the author or her book by any company, organization, or owner of any brand.

First published in the United States by St. Martin's Griffin, an imprint of St. Martin's Publishing Group

www.stmartins.com

Book design by Ralph Fowler
Illustrations by Jack Pullan
Food styling by Natalie Drobny
Food photography by Jennifer Davick

The Library of Congress Cataloging-in-Publication Data is available upon request.

ISBN 978-1-250-31094-1 (trade paperback)
ISBN 978-1-250-31095-8 (ebook)

Our books may be purchased in bulk for promotional, educational, or business use. Please contact your local bookseller or the Macmillan Corporate and Premium Sales Department at 1-800-221-7945, extension 5442, or by email at MacmillanSpecialMarkets@macmillan.com.

First Edition: 2022

10 9 8 7 6 5 4 3 2 1

contents

Blueberry
Crumble
Oatmeal,
page 22

slow-cooker
recipes

oatmeal

breakfast casseroles

soups

Chicken & Cauli Rice Soup, page 36

chilis

apps & sides

meal starters

Classic Macaroni & Cheese, page 110

casseroles

pasta

entrées

Homestyle Meatloaf, page 149

desserts

air-fryer recipes

bagels & bagel bites

French Toast Sticks, page 188

more breakfast dishes

apps & sides

small bites

burgers, wraps & sandwiches

Pretzel-Coated Pork
Tenderloin, page 289

pizzas & calzones

entrées

desserts

Apple Cranberry
Cobbler Cake, page 151

acknowledgments

This feel-good recipe collection is the result of lots of hard work. Tremendous thank-yous to . . .

Jamie Goldberg—16 years and 15 books later, you're still THE BEST and a complete lifesaver. THANK YOU for always having my back and for being the super glue that holds everything together.

The too-talented-for-words Hungry Girl book team—you are INCREDIBLE!

Lynn Bettencourt	Erin Norcross	Amanda Maisonet
Dana DeRuyck	Allie Benish	Katie Killeavy

Special thanks to these HG team members for all they do to keep our Hungry world running so successfully . . .

Peggy Mansfield	Mike Sherry	Samantha Vazio	Olga Gatica

And to my extended Hungry Girl family . . .

John Vaccaro	Brant Janeway	James Sinclair	Steve Younger
Neeti Madan	Erica Martirano	Lena Shekhter	Jeff Becker
Jennifer Enderlin	Elizabeth Catalano	Tracey Guest	Susan Garcia
John Karle	Michael Clark	Bill Stankey	
Anne Marie Tallberg	Christina Lopez	Tom Fineman	

These creative folks deserve kudos for making the book so beautiful . . .

Ralph Fowler	Jennifer Davick	Natalie Drobny	Jack Pullan

Finally, much love and gratitude to my family . . .

Daniel Schneider	Jay Lillien
Florence and Maurice Lillien	Lolly, Bam Bam, and Jordan
Meri Lillien	

introduction

Hi there!

When I was in second grade, my teacher gave us an assignment to write a book. I decided to write a mystery called *The Robbery at Liberty Savings Bank*. This book had it all: interesting characters, wonderful illustrations (that I personally drew), twists and turns (like any good mystery), a cardboard cover coated with hideously colorful contact paper, and (of course) a simple About the Author page. The copy read, "Lisa Lillien was born in Brooklyn, New York. She likes to swim and write books. This is her first book." Little did I know that there would be many more published works to come. And while this book is not a page-turning mystery, one could argue that the fact that there have been 14 Hungry Girl cookbooks published and not a single one has been devoted to comfort food is a mystery in and of itself.

Simply Comfort changes that. This is a book devoted to foods that taste great and make us feel good, a.k.a. comfort foods (which happen to be my personal favorites). The added bonus is that all of these recipes are intended to be made in either a slow cooker or an air fryer. Slow-cooker recipes have always been in demand in the Hungry Girl world. And air-fryer recipes, while a lot newer, keep growing and growing in popularity. Over the past two years, my air fryer has easily become the MVP of my kitchen. Of course, if you choose not to use these appliances and prefer making them with a traditional oven, there are easy ways to make that happen.

Dumplings, wraps, bagels, apps, meatloaves, mashies! Soups, stews, casseroles, chilis, pastas, and decadent desserts! They're all here, and so much more! A whopping 200 easy, delicious recipes that'll not only satisfy you but make you feel GREAT, too. Enjoy . . .

Happy chewing!!!
Lisa

Southwest Chicken Empanadas, page 244

FAQs

Can I make these recipes without an air fryer or slow cooker?

Good news: YES! While the recipes in this book were developed to be made in air fryers and slow cookers, they can easily be made in ovens or on stoves instead. At the beginning of each section of the book, you'll find everything you need to know to seamlessly translate the recipes for baking and stovetop cooking—flip to page 16 for the slow cooker 411, and get the air-fryer info on page 173.

Are these recipes all natural?

Yes! These recipes mostly call for "whole" natural ingredients. Think lean protein, fruit, veggies, eggs, and more. Any other ingredients—like cheese, condiments, or canned goods—are readily available in stores in natural varieties without anything artificial added. When in doubt, look for trusted natural brands or shop at a natural foods store.

Are these recipes good for weight loss or meant for a specific diet?

Most of these recipes are high in protein and fiber, and they're low in starchy carbs, added sugars, and calories. They won't magically make you lose weight, but they'll fill you up without weighing you down, and they fit perfectly into many weight-loss plans.

As a "foodologist" (remember, I'm not a nutrition professional), I don't offer medical advice related to dietary conditions. But what I do provide is full nutritional information carefully calculated for each and every recipe. Feel free to modify them and make them work for you!

Where can I find the WW points values?

To support anyone on a WW journey, I calculate the points values for all Hungry Girl recipes. At WW's request, and because the points system changes from time to time, I don't include these values in Hungry Girl cookbooks. But I DO provide the recipe values online. Visit hungry-girl.com/comfort for the WW points values* of the recipes in this book.

*The points values for these recipes were calculated by Hungry Girl and are not an endorsement or approval of the recipe or its developer by WW International, Inc., the owner of these trademarks.

recipe guide

As you read through this book, look for the symbols below for an at-a-glance snapshot of the recipe's attributes. Even more helpful? The recipes in each category are listed on the following pages, along with their page numbers for easy reference!

5i Recipes with 5 Ingredients or Less

15m Recipes in 15 Minutes or Less

30m Recipes in 30 Minutes or Less

V Vegetarian Recipes

GF Gluten-Free Recipes

Shredded Salsa Verde Chicken, page 89

5i

recipes with 5 ingredients or less

It's true: Each of these recipes calls for five main ingredients max!
(Basic seasonings, ice, and water don't count.)

Pistachio-Crusted Mahi Mahi, page 290

15m

recipes in 15 minutes or less

Make these super-speedy recipes your go-tos for quick breakfasts, fast apps, and last-minute lunches . . .

recipes in 30 minutes or less

While you won't find any slow-cooker recipes on this list (that would kind of defeat the purpose!), here are some fast air-fryer recipes . . .

vegetarian recipes

Whether you follow a 100 percent vegetarian diet or you're just looking to add more meatless options to your rotation, these are the recipes for you . . .

California Breakfast Burrito, page 199

gluten-free recipes

Gluten avoiders: No need to scour the pages of this cookbook looking to see which recipes work for you. You'll find them all on this convenient list . . .

HG Heads-Up
Naturally gluten-free foods may contain a hint of gluten due to cross contamination. And occasionally, brands will add gluten to products (like seasoning mixes) that are otherwise gluten free. If you're sensitive to gluten, read labels carefully.

Caramelized Bananas, page 167

Scoopable Classic Lasagna,
page 105

slow-cooker *recipes*

Welcome to the wonderful world of Hungry Girl slow-cooker recipes: your set-it-and-forget-it solution for healthy meals at your fingertips. **You'll find 100 of my favorite easy creations on the following pages**—from breakfast to dessert, and everything in between! But first, here's some need-to-know info . . .

slow-cooking 101

Size matters. These recipes were developed for standard slow cookers with a 4–6 quart capacity. These days, you'll find slow cookers as small as 1 quart and as large as 10 quarts. If using a smaller or larger slow cooker, you may need to divide or multiply the ingredient quantities and adjust the cook time. A good guideline: Slow cookers work best when they're at least half full. Any less and the food may burn. Overfilling could lead to undercooking your food or cooking it unevenly.

Make cleanup easy. Always spray your slow cooker generously with nonstick spray. (The exception is when making broth-based soups.) Two other fantastic options: slow-cooker liners and aluminum foil. The liners are disposable, heat-resistant plastic bags designed to fit right in your slow cooker—no spray needed. When using foil to line your slow cooker, I recommend a nice mist of nonstick spray.

Top tip: Don't peek. Resist the urge to remove the lid while your food is cooking. You really want to let the slow cooker work its magic, without releasing any of that heat and steam. It works best if you just let it be during the cook time, unless instructed otherwise.

Fun fact: The Instant Pot works as a slow cooker! In addition to its pressure-cooker functions, Instant Pots have slow-cooker settings and will work perfectly for these recipes. So if you've been debating whether to buy a standard slow cooker or an Instant Pot, this might be the sign you need.

P.S. These recipes can be made even if you don't have a slow cooker or Instant Pot. Flip to page 16 for all the info on converting these recipes to oven-baked creations or stovetop sensations.

Creamy Tomato Basil Soup, page 31

Broc 'n Cheese Soup, page 29

Slow-cooker recipes are fantastic for make-ahead meals and heat & eat leftovers. But before you toss them in the freezer willy-nilly, here's some helpful info . . .

Most (but not all) of these recipes will freeze, thaw, and reheat well. Oatmeal, casseroles, soups, chilis, entrées, and more all pass the test. When it comes to casseroles, just avoid freezing anything with a dough-based topping. It's also a good idea to slightly undercook pasta dishes if you plan to freeze them. Dessert recipes generally don't freeze well, but they're so good they probably won't even last long enough to freeze!

Ready to get freezing? First things first: Divvy up the food into equal servings using containers that are freezer safe and microwave friendly. Choose containers a little larger than the serving itself since food expands when it freezes. Next, let it cool completely so what's already in your freezer doesn't start to thaw from the heat. Then just seal it up. **HG Tip:** Label containers with the date and the contents!

Ready to reheat? If possible, thaw your food in the fridge overnight. This way, all you'll have to do is remove or vent the lid and microwave for a few minutes! If you didn't thaw the food in advance, remove/vent the lid and use the defrost setting on your microwave. Check on it and give it a stir every minute or two, until it reaches your desired temperature.

Jalapeño Cheddar Turkey Chili, page 61

oven & stovetop conversion chart ✦✗

Use the below guide to determine the ideal time for your dish to cook. But first, a few pointers.

Oatmeals, soups, stews, and chilis cook best on the stove. Bring them to a boil, and then reduce to a simmer before setting your timer.

Dishes like casseroles and entrées generally perform well at 350°F. For meatloaves, use a loaf pan. For dishes that serve four, an 8-inch by 8-inch pan will often do the trick. Dishes that serve five or more are often best suited for a 9-inch by 13-inch pan.

Put a lid on it. Whether you're cooking on the stove or in the oven, cover the pot or pan with a lid to mimic the slow-cooker process, locking in the steam and flavor.

Adjust liquid ingredients as needed. Since slow cookers use lower temperatures, liquids don't reduce as much. When you transition these recipes to the oven or stove, increase your liquid by about 30 percent. For example, if a recipe calls for 3 cups of broth, up that to 4 cups.

Slow Cooker on High	Slow Cooker on Low	Stovetop or Oven
1–3 hours	2–6 hours	15–30 minutes
3–5 hours	6–9 hours	35–60 minutes

A few exceptions . . . Cobbler cakes and dump cakes take a little longer in the oven: Allow up to 1 hour at 350°F. The scoopable pies will take 15–30 minutes on the stove.

As with any recipe, these times are just estimates. Individual results may vary. Always check that your food is fully cooked before serving. Refer to the recipe indicators—like "until chicken is fully cooked and veggies are tender"—to determine when the recipe is ready.

And now, the recipes . . .

 *oatmeal*

classic growing oatmeal

Pictured on pages 20–21

2 cups unsweetened vanilla almond milk
2 cups old-fashioned oats
5 packets natural no-calorie sweetener
1 tablespoon vanilla extract
2 teaspoons cinnamon
¼ teaspoon salt
Optional topping: fresh fruit

1. Spray a slow cooker with nonstick spray. Add all ingredients and 4 cups water. Mix well.

2. Cover and cook on low for 2½ hours, or until mostly thick and creamy.

3. Turn off slow cooker. Vent lid slightly, and let sit for 30 minutes, or until thickened.

4. Stir before serving.

MAKES 4 SERVINGS

185 calories

Prep: 5 minutes

Cook: 2½ hours

Cool: 30 minutes

You'll Need: slow cooker, nonstick spray

¼ of recipe (about 1½ cups):
185 calories
4g total fat
(0.5g sat. fat)
235mg sodium
30.5g carbs
5g fiber
1.5g sugars
6g protein

HG FYI
The extra liquid makes the serving size GROW as it cools and thickens!

bananaberry growing oatmeal

Pictured on pages 20–21

2 cups unsweetened vanilla almond milk
2 cups old-fashioned oats
1 cup (about 2 medium) mashed extra-ripe bananas
4 packets natural no-calorie sweetener
1 tablespoon vanilla extract
2 teaspoons cinnamon
¼ teaspoon salt
1½ cups chopped freeze-dried strawberries, divided
Optional topping: fresh strawberries

1. Spray a slow cooker with nonstick spray. Add all ingredients except freeze-dried strawberries.

2. Add 3 cups water and 1 cup freeze-dried strawberries. Mix well.

3. Cover and cook on low for 2½ hours, or until mostly thick and creamy.

4. Turn off slow cooker. Vent lid slightly, and let sit for 30 minutes, or until thickened.

5. Stir before serving. Top each portion with 2 tablespoons of the remaining freeze-dried strawberries.

MAKES 4 SERVINGS

274 calories

Prep: 10 minutes

Cook: 2½ hours

Cool: 30 minutes

You'll Need: slow cooker, nonstick spray

¼ of recipe (about 1½ cups):
274 calories
4.5g total fat
(0.5g sat. fat)
235mg sodium
51.5g carbs
8.5g fiber
14g sugars
6.5g protein

apple maple protein oatmeal

Pictured on pages 20–21

⅓ cup plain protein powder with about 100 calories per scoop
2 cups unsweetened vanilla almond milk
2 cups chopped Fuji or Gala apples, or more for topping
1 cup steel-cut oats
5 packets natural no-calorie sweetener
1½ tablespoons chia seeds
2 teaspoons cinnamon
2 teaspoons maple extract
½ teaspoon vanilla extract
¼ teaspoon salt

1. Spray a slow cooker with nonstick spray. Add protein powder and 2 cups warm water. Whisk until uniform.

2. Add remaining ingredients. Mix well.

3. Cover and cook on high for 3–4 hours or on low for 7–8 hours, until oats have cooked, liquid has been absorbed, and apples have softened.

MAKES 4 SERVINGS

262 calories

Prep: 10 minutes

Cook: 3–4 hours or 7–8 hours

You'll Need: slow cooker, nonstick spray, whisk

¼ of recipe (about 1¼ cups):
262 calories
6g total fat
(0.5g sat. fat)
247mg sodium
41.5g carbs
9.5g fiber
7.5g sugars
12.5g protein

BananaBerry Growing
Oatmeal, page 18

Apple Maple Protein
Oatmeal, page 19

Blueberry
Crumble
Oatmeal,
page 22

Classic Growing
Oatmeal,
page 17

blueberry crumble oatmeal

Pictured on pages 20–21

2 cups unsweetened vanilla almond milk
1 cup steel-cut oats
5 packets natural no-calorie sweetener
1½ tablespoons chia seeds
2 teaspoons cinnamon
2 teaspoons vanilla extract
¼ teaspoon plus 1 dash salt, divided
¼ teaspoon ground nutmeg
¼ teaspoon almond extract
2 cups blueberries (fresh or thawed from frozen), divided
¼ cup old-fashioned oats
1 tablespoon whole wheat flour
1½ tablespoons brown sugar
1½ tablespoons whipped butter

1. Spray a slow cooker with nonstick spray. Add milk, steel-cut oats, sweetener, chia seeds, cinnamon, vanilla extract, ¼ teaspoon salt, nutmeg, and almond extract. Add 1 cup blueberries and 2 cups water. Mix well.

2. Cover and cook on high for 3–4 hours or on low for 7–8 hours, until oats have cooked and liquid has been absorbed.

3. To make the crumble topping, combine old-fashioned oats, flour, brown sugar, butter, and remaining 1 dash salt in a small microwave-safe bowl. Mash and stir until well mixed. Microwave for 45 seconds. Stir well. Microwave for 45 more seconds, or until crumbly.

4. Just before serving, top each portion with ¼ cup of the remaining blueberries and about 1½ tablespoons of the crumble topping.

MAKES 4 SERVINGS

316 calories

Prep: 5 minutes

Cook: 3–4 hours or 7–8 hours

You'll Need: slow cooker, nonstick spray, small microwave-safe bowl

¼ of recipe (about 1 cup oatmeal plus topping):
316 calories
8.5g total fat
(2g sat. fat)
294mg sodium
51g carbs
10g fiber
11.5g sugars
8.5g protein

breakfast casseroles

three-cheese breakfast casserole

Pictured on pages 26–27

4 cups frozen shredded hash browns, divided
½ cup shredded reduced-fat cheddar cheese, divided
½ cup shredded part-skim mozzarella cheese, divided
4 cups (about 32 large) egg whites or fat-free liquid egg substitute
⅓ cup unsweetened plain almond milk
¼ cup whipped cream cheese
½ teaspoon garlic powder
¼ teaspoon salt
¼ teaspoon black pepper
Optional toppings: light sour cream, chopped scallions

1. Fully line a slow cooker with heavy-duty aluminum foil, draping several inches of excess foil over the sides. (You'll use the draped foil to lift out the cooked casserole.) Spray with nonstick spray.

2. Add 2 cups hash browns to the slow cooker in an even layer. Top with ¼ cup cheddar cheese and ¼ cup mozzarella cheese. Add remaining 2 cups hash browns in an even layer.

3. In a large bowl, combine egg whites/substitute, milk, cream cheese, and seasonings. Whisk thoroughly. Evenly pour mixture over the contents of the slow cooker.

4. Cover and cook on high for 3–4 hours or on low for 7–8 hours, until egg layer is cooked through.

5. Turn off slow cooker. Top casserole with remaining ¼ cup cheddar cheese and ¼ cup mozzarella cheese. Cover and let sit for 5 minutes, or until cheese has melted.

6. Using the foil, lift casserole out of the slow cooker and onto a cutting board to cut before serving.

MAKES 6 SERVINGS

205 calories

Prep: 10 minutes

Cook: 3–4 hours
or 7–8 hours, plus
5 minutes

You'll Need: slow cooker, heavy-duty aluminum foil, nonstick spray, large bowl, whisk, cutting board

⅙ of recipe:
205 calories
5.5g total fat
(3g sat. fat)
613mg sodium
13g carbs
1g fiber
0.5g sugars
22.5g protein

all-american breakfast casserole

Pictured on pages 26–27

3 frozen meatless or turkey sausage patties with 80 calories or less
2 cups frozen shredded hash browns
1 cup shredded reduced-fat Mexican-blend cheese, divided
3 cups frozen riced cauliflower, thawed and drained
¾ cup chopped bell pepper, or more for topping
¾ cup chopped onion
2½ cups (about 20 large) egg whites or fat-free liquid egg substitute
⅓ cup unsweetened plain almond milk
½ teaspoon garlic powder
¼ teaspoon salt
¼ teaspoon black pepper
Optional toppings: salsa, light sour cream

1. Prepare sausage patties in a skillet sprayed with nonstick spray or on a microwave-safe plate in the microwave. (See package for cook time.) Once cool enough to handle, crumble or chop.

2. Fully line a slow cooker with heavy-duty aluminum foil, draping several inches of excess foil over the sides. (You'll use the draped foil to lift out the cooked casserole.) Spray with nonstick spray.

3. Add hash browns to the slow cooker in an even layer. Top with sausage, ¾ cup cheese, cauliflower, bell pepper, and onion.

4. In a large bowl, combine egg whites/substitute, milk, and seasonings. Whisk thoroughly. Pour mixture over the contents of the slow cooker.

5. Cover and cook on high for 3–4 hours or on low for 7–8 hours, until egg layer is cooked through.

6. Turn off slow cooker. Top casserole with remaining ¼ cup cheese. Cover and let sit for 5 minutes, or until cheese has melted.

7. Using the foil, lift casserole out of the slow cooker and onto a cutting board to cut before serving.

MAKES 6 SERVINGS

203 calories

Prep: 15 minutes

Cook: 3–4 hours or 7–8 hours, plus 5 minutes

You'll Need: skillet or microwave-safe plate, nonstick spray, slow cooker, heavy-duty aluminum foil, large bowl, whisk, cutting board

⅙ of recipe:
203 calories
5.5g total fat
(3g sat. fat)
597mg sodium
15g carbs
3g fiber
3g sugars
21.5g protein

denver omelette casserole

Pictured on pages 26–27

1 cup chopped green bell pepper
1 cup chopped onion
4 ounces (about 6 slices) reduced-sodium ham, chopped
½ cup shredded reduced-fat cheddar cheese, divided
4 cups (about 32 large) egg whites or fat-free liquid egg substitute
⅓ cup unsweetened plain almond milk
¼ cup whipped cream cheese
½ teaspoon garlic powder
½ teaspoon onion powder
Optional toppings: chopped scallions, light sour cream, tomato slices

1. Fully line a slow cooker with heavy-duty aluminum foil, draping several inches of excess foil over the sides. (You'll use the draped foil to lift out the cooked casserole.) Spray with nonstick spray.

2. Add pepper and onion in an even layer. Top with ham and ¼ cup cheddar cheese.

3. In a large bowl, combine egg whites/substitute, milk, cream cheese, garlic powder, and onion powder. Whisk thoroughly. Pour mixture over the contents of the slow cooker.

4. Cover and cook on high for 3–4 hours or on low for 7–8 hours, until egg layer is cooked through.

5. Turn off slow cooker. Top casserole with remaining ¼ cup cheddar cheese. Cover and let sit for 5 minutes, or until cheese has melted.

6. Using the foil, lift casserole out of the slow cooker and onto a cutting board to cut before serving.

MAKES 6 SERVINGS

170 calories

 GF

Prep: 10 minutes

Cook: 3–4 hours or 7–8 hours, plus 5 minutes

You'll Need: slow cooker, heavy-duty aluminum foil, nonstick spray, large bowl, whisk, cutting board

⅙ of recipe:
170 calories
4g total fat
(2g sat. fat)
541mg sodium
7.5g carbs
1g fiber
2.5g sugars
23.5g protein

Denver Omelette
Casserole, page 25

Three-Cheese Breakfast
Casserole, page 23

Sun-Dried Tomato & Feta
Breakfast Casserole, page 28

All-American
Breakfast
Casserole,
page 24

sun-dried tomato & feta breakfast casserole

Pictured on pages 26–27

6 cups chopped spinach

4 cups (about 32 large) egg whites or fat-free liquid egg substitute

⅓ cup unsweetened plain almond milk

¼ cup whipped cream cheese

½ teaspoon garlic powder

¼ teaspoon salt

⅛ teaspoon black pepper

½ cup bagged or drained sun-dried tomatoes, chopped

½ cup crumbled feta cheese

1. Fully line a slow cooker with heavy-duty aluminum foil, draping several inches of excess foil over the sides. (You'll use the draped foil to lift out the cooked casserole.) Spray with nonstick spray.

2. Spray a skillet with nonstick spray, and bring to medium heat. Add spinach, and cook and stir until wilted, about 2 minutes. Drain/blot away excess moisture.

3. In a large bowl, combine egg whites/substitute, milk, cream cheese, and seasonings. Whisk thoroughly. Add tomatoes, feta, and cooked spinach. Stir well. Transfer mixture to the slow cooker.

4. Cover and cook on high for 3–4 hours or on low for 7–8 hours, until cooked through.

5. Using the foil, lift casserole out of the slow cooker and onto a cutting board to cut before serving.

MAKES 6 SERVINGS

165 calories

Prep: 10 minutes

Cook: 5 minutes, plus 3–4 hours or 7–8 hours

You'll Need: slow cooker, heavy-duty aluminum foil, nonstick spray, skillet, large bowl, whisk, cutting board

⅙ of recipe:
165 calories
3.5g total fat
(2.5g sat. fat)
577mg sodium
9g carbs
2g fiber
3.5g sugars
21g protein

soups

broc 'n cheese soup

Pictured on pages 32–33

5 cups chopped cauliflower
4 cups chopped broccoli
3 cups vegetable broth
1 teaspoon garlic powder
1 teaspoon onion powder
¼ teaspoon salt
¼ teaspoon black pepper
½ cup shredded reduced-fat cheddar cheese
½ cup light/reduced-fat cream cheese

1. Place all ingredients except cheddar cheese and cream cheese in a slow cooker. Mix well.

2. Cover and cook on high for 2–3 hours or on low for 5–6 hours, until veggies are tender.

3. Using a slotted spoon, transfer half of the veggies to a blender. Add cheddar cheese, cream cheese, and 1 cup of the liquid from the slow cooker. Puree until smooth.

4. Return pureed mixture to the slow cooker. Mix well.

MAKES 6 SERVINGS

125 calories

Prep: 15 minutes

Cook: 2–3 hours or 5–6 hours

You'll Need: slow cooker, slotted spoon

⅙ of recipe (about 1 cup):
125 calories
6.5g total fat
(3.5g sat. fat)
654mg sodium
11.5g carbs
3.5g fiber
4.5g sugars
7.5g protein

black bean corn chowder

Pictured on pages 32–33

3 cups vegetable broth
One 15-ounce can black beans, drained and rinsed
One 14.75-ounce can cream-style corn
1 cup frozen sweet corn kernels
1 cup chopped red bell pepper
1 cup chopped onion
½ cup fat-free milk
2 teaspoons chopped garlic
1 teaspoon ground cumin
½ teaspoon salt
½ cup instant mashed potato flakes
⅓ cup light sour cream
¼ cup chopped fresh cilantro, or more for topping

1. Place all ingredients except potato flakes, sour cream, and cilantro in a slow cooker. Mix well.

2. Cover and cook on high for 3–4 hours or on low for 7–8 hours, until veggies are tender.

3. Stir in potato flakes, sour cream, and cilantro.

MAKES 8 SERVINGS

143 calories

Prep: 10 minutes

Cook: 3–4 hours or 7–8 hours

You'll Need: slow cooker

⅛ of recipe (about 1 cup):
143 calories
1.5g total fat
(0.5g sat. fat)
713mg sodium
27g carbs
4.5g fiber
8.5g sugars
5.5g protein

creamy tomato basil soup

Pictured on pages 32–33

Two 28-ounce cans whole tomatoes (not drained)
2 cups roughly chopped carrots
1 cup roughly chopped onion
¼ cup chopped fresh basil, or more for topping
1 tablespoon chopped garlic
1 teaspoon dried oregano
¼ teaspoon salt
¼ teaspoon black pepper
½ cup light sour cream

1. Add tomatoes to a slow cooker. Break them up with a spoon or potato masher.

2. Add 1 cup water and all remaining ingredients except sour cream. Mix well.

3. Cover and cook on high for 3–4 hours or on low for 7–8 hours, until veggies are tender.

4. Using a slotted spoon, transfer veggies to a blender. Add sour cream, and puree until smooth.

5. Return pureed mixture to the slow cooker. Mix well.

MAKES 6 SERVINGS

117 calories

Prep: 15 minutes

Cook: 3–4 hours or 7–8 hours

You'll Need: slow cooker, potato masher (optional), slotted spoon, blender

⅙ of recipe (about 1¼ cups):
117 calories
2g total fat
(1g sat. fat)
490mg sodium
20.5g carbs
5g fiber
12.5g sugars
4g protein

HG Tip
Leave out the sour cream to please vegan taste buds. . . Still delicious!

HG Alternative
Instead of transferring the veggies to a standard blender, use an immersion (a.k.a. stick) blender to puree them right in the slow cooker.

Super-Hearty Lentil
Soup, page 34

Black Bean Corn Chowder,
page 30

Moroccan Vegetable Stew, page 35

Broc 'n Cheese Soup, page 29

Creamy Tomato Basil Soup, page 31

super-hearty lentil soup

Pictured on pages 32–33

6 cups vegetable broth

One 14-ounce can crushed tomatoes

2 cups dry green or brown lentils

2 cups chopped mushrooms

2 cups chopped onion

1½ cups chopped carrots

1 tablespoon chopped garlic

1 teaspoon smoked paprika

½ teaspoon ground cumin

2 bay leaves

3 cups chopped spinach

¼ cup grated Parmesan cheese

1 tablespoon lemon juice

Optional topping: shaved Parmesan cheese

254 calories

Prep: 15 minutes

Cook: 3–4 hours
or 7–8 hours, plus
5 minutes

Cool: 10 minutes

You'll Need: slow
cooker, blender

**⅛ of recipe
(about 1⅓ cups):**
254 calories
2g total fat
(1g sat. fat)
745mg sodium
43.5g carbs
8.5g fiber
7.5g sugars
16.5g protein

1. In a slow cooker, combine all ingredients except spinach, Parm, and lemon juice. Mix well.

2. Cover and cook on high for 3–4 hours or on low for 7–8 hours, until veggies are tender and lentils are cooked.

3. If cooking at high heat, reduce to low. Remove and discard bay leaves. Transfer 4 cups of the soup to a blender. Let cool, about 10 minutes.

4. Meanwhile, add spinach, Parm, and lemon juice to the slow cooker. Mix well.

5. Pulse soup in the blender until mostly smooth. Return pureed soup to the slow cooker. Mix well. Cover and cook for 5 minutes, or until hot.

MAKES 8 SERVINGS

HG FYI
Most Parmesan cheese isn't vegetarian.
Feel free to leave it out for a strictly
vegetarian soup.

moroccan vegetable stew

Pictured on pages 32–33

2 cups roughly chopped bell pepper

2 cups roughly chopped broccoli

2 cups cubed butternut squash

One 15-ounce can crushed tomatoes

One 14.5-ounce can chickpeas, drained and rinsed

1 cup roughly chopped onion

2 tablespoons tomato paste

1 tablespoon chopped garlic

½ teaspoon ground cumin

½ teaspoon smoked paprika

¼ teaspoon cinnamon

¼ teaspoon ground ginger

1. Add all ingredients to a slow cooker. Mix well.

2. Cover and cook on high for 3–4 hours or on low for 7–8 hours, until veggies are tender.

MAKES 4 SERVINGS

226 calories

Prep: 10 minutes

Cook: 3–4 hours or 7–8 hours

You'll Need: slow cooker

¼ of recipe (about 1½ cups):
226 calories
2g total fat
(0g sat. fat)
417mg sodium
44g carbs
12g fiber
12g sugars
10.5g protein

chicken & cauli rice soup

Pictured on opposite page

1 pound raw boneless skinless chicken breasts
¼ teaspoon salt
¼ teaspoon black pepper
6 cups chicken broth
2 cups chopped carrots
1 cup chopped celery
1 cup chopped onion
2 teaspoons chopped garlic
2 bay leaves
½ teaspoon onion powder
¼ teaspoon ground thyme
2 cups frozen riced cauliflower

1. Place chicken in a slow cooker, and season with salt and pepper. Add all remaining ingredients except cauliflower. Mix well.

2. Cover and cook on high for 3–4 hours or on low for 7–8 hours, until veggies are tender and chicken is fully cooked.

3. Turn off slow cooker. Remove and discard bay leaves. Transfer chicken to a large bowl, and shred with two forks.

4. Return chicken to the slow cooker. Add cauliflower. Mix well. Cover and let sit for 5–10 minutes, until hot.

MAKES 10 SERVINGS

87 calories

Prep: 15 minutes

Cook: 3–4 hours or 7–8 hours, plus 10 minutes

You'll Need: slow cooker, large bowl

¹⁄₁₀ of recipe (about 1 cup):
87 calories
1.5g total fat
(<0.5g sat. fat)
587mg sodium
6.5g carbs
1.5g fiber
3g sugars
11.5g protein

Chicken & Cauli Rice
Soup, opposite page

Chicken Enchilada
Soup, page 40

Creamy Chicken
Noodle Soup,
page 39

Chicken Tortilla
Soup, page 38

chicken tortilla soup

Pictured on page 37

Soup

1 pound raw boneless skinless chicken breasts
1½ tablespoons taco seasoning
4 cups chicken broth
One 14.5-ounce can fire-roasted diced tomatoes (not drained)
1½ cups chopped onion
1 cup chopped bell pepper
2 tablespoons seeded and finely chopped jalapeño pepper
1 tablespoon lime juice
½ teaspoon garlic powder
½ teaspoon onion powder

Tortilla Strips

Four 6-inch corn tortillas
¼ teaspoon ground cumin
¼ teaspoon chili powder

Topping

4 ounces (about ½ cup) chopped avocado

1. Place chicken in a slow cooker. Season with ½ tablespoon taco seasoning.

2. Add chicken broth and all remaining soup ingredients, including remaining 1 tablespoon taco seasoning. Mix well.

3. Cover and cook on high for 3–4 hours or on low for 7–8 hours, until chicken is fully cooked.

4. Meanwhile, prepare tortilla strips. Preheat oven to 400°F. Spray a baking sheet with nonstick spray. Cut tortillas into thin 2-inch-long strips, and lay on the baking sheet. Lightly spray with nonstick spray, and top with seasonings. Bake until crispy, about 8 minutes, flipping halfway through.

5. Transfer chicken to a large bowl. Shred with two forks. Return chicken to the slow cooker. Mix well.

6. Serve topped with tortilla strips and avocado.

MAKES 8 SERVINGS

155 calories

Prep: 20 minutes

Cook: 3–4 hours or 7–8 hours

You'll Need: slow cooker, baking sheet, nonstick spray, large bowl

⅛ of recipe (about 1 cup plus toppings):
155 calories
4g total fat
(0.5g sat. fat)
600mg sodium
14g carbs
3g fiber
4g sugars
15g protein

HG Heads Up
Not all taco seasonings are gluten free, so read labels carefully if that's a concern.

creamy chicken noodle soup

Pictured on page 37

1 pound raw boneless skinless chicken breasts
¼ teaspoon salt
¼ teaspoon black pepper
4 cups reduced-sodium chicken broth
1 cup thinly sliced carrots
1 cup chopped celery
1 cup chopped onion
2 teaspoons chopped garlic
¼ teaspoon ground thyme
1 bay leaf
½ cup light/reduced-fat cream cheese
½ cup instant mashed potato flakes
4½ ounces (about 2 cups) uncooked wide egg noodles

1. Place chicken in a slow cooker, and season with salt and pepper. Add all remaining ingredients except cream cheese, potato flakes, and noodles. Mix well.

2. Cover and cook on high for 3–4 hours or on low for 7–8 hours, until chicken is fully cooked.

3. Discard bay leaf. Transfer chicken to a large bowl. Shred with two forks.

4. Return chicken to the slow cooker. Add cream cheese and potato flakes. Mix until uniform. Stir in noodles.

5. If cooking at low heat, increase to high. Cover and cook for 10 minutes, or until noodles are tender.

MAKES 8 SERVINGS

203 calories

Prep: 10 minutes

Cook: 3–4 hours or 7–8 hours, plus 10 minutes

You'll Need: slow cooker, large bowl

⅛ of recipe (about 1 cup):
203 calories
5g total fat
(2.5g sat. fat)
472mg sodium
20.5g carbs
2g fiber
3g sugars
17.5g protein

soup tip!

Some soups thicken once refrigerated for a day or more. Feel free to add additional broth or water as needed when reheating.

chicken enchilada soup

Pictured on page 37

3 cups low-sodium chicken broth
2 cups red enchilada sauce
One 15-ounce can black beans, drained and rinsed
One 15-ounce can pure pumpkin
1 cup frozen sweet corn kernels
1 cup finely chopped onion
One 4-ounce can diced green chiles (not drained)
1 pound raw boneless skinless chicken breasts
Optional toppings: shredded reduced-fat cheddar cheese, light sour cream, fresh cilantro

1. Place all ingredients except chicken in a slow cooker. Mix until uniform.

2. Add chicken. Cover and cook on high for 4–5 hours or on low for 8–9 hours, until chicken is fully cooked.

3. Transfer chicken to a large bowl. Shred with two forks. Return chicken to the slow cooker. Mix well.

MAKES 10 SERVINGS

145 calories

Prep: 10 minutes

Cook: 4–5 hours or 8–9 hours

You'll Need: slow cooker, large bowl

¹⁄₁₀ of recipe (about 1 cup):
145 calories
2g total fat
(<0.5g sat. fat)
431mg sodium
17g carbs
4g fiber
4g sugars
14g protein

new england clam chowder

Pictured on page 42

4 cups roughly chopped cauliflower
14 ounces (about 2 medium) white potatoes, peeled and cubed
1 cup chopped onion
1 cup chopped celery
3 cups reduced-sodium chicken broth
1½ tablespoons chopped garlic
¼ teaspoon black pepper
2 cups fat-free milk
½ cup instant mashed potato flakes
Two 10-ounce cans baby clams (not drained)

1. Place all ingredients except milk, potato flakes, and clams in a slow cooker. Mix well.

2. Cover and cook on high for 3–4 hours or on low for 7–8 hours, until veggies are tender.

3. Using a slotted spoon, transfer about half of the cooked veggies to a blender. Add milk. Puree until smooth.

4. Return pureed mixture to the slow cooker. Add potato flakes, and mix until uniform. Stir in clams. Cover and cook for 5 minutes, or until hot.

MAKES 10 SERVINGS

115 calories

Prep: 10 minutes

Cook: 3–4 hours or 7–8 hours, plus 5 minutes

You'll Need: slow cooker, slotted spoon, blender

¹⁄₁₀ of recipe (about 1 cups):
115 calories
<0.5g total fat
(0g sat. fat)
510mg sodium
18.5g carbs
2g fiber
4.5g sugars
10g protein

Manhattan
Clam Chowder,
opposite page

New England Clam
Chowder, page 41

manhattan clam chowder

Pictured on opposite page

One 29-ounce can crushed tomatoes
One 14.5-ounce can diced tomatoes (not drained)
1½ cups chopped onion
1 cup chicken broth
1 cup chopped carrots
1 cup chopped celery
8 ounces (about 1 medium) russet potato, peeled and cubed
1 teaspoon ground thyme
¼ teaspoon black pepper
Two 10-ounce cans baby clams (not drained)
Optional: fresh parsley

1. Place all ingredients except clams in a slow cooker. Mix well.

2. Cover and cook on high for 3–4 hours or on low for 7–8 hours, until veggies are tender.

3. Turn off slow cooker. Mix in clams.

MAKES 10 SERVINGS

100 calories

 GF

Prep: 10 minutes

Cook: 3–4 hours or 7–8 hours

You'll Need: slow cooker

¹⁄₁₀ of recipe (about 1 cup):
100 calories
<0.5g total fat
(0g sat. fat)
635mg sodium
17.5g carbs
3.5g fiber
6g sugars
8g protein

beef barley soup

Pictured on pages 48–49

1½ pounds lean beef stew meat, cut into bite-sized pieces
½ teaspoon salt
¼ teaspoon black pepper
6 cups reduced-sodium beef broth
2 cups chopped carrots
1 cup chopped celery
1 cup chopped onion
2 tablespoons tomato paste
2 teaspoons garlic
1 teaspoon chopped fresh rosemary
2 bay leaves
1 cup uncooked pearl barley
Optional topping: grated Parmesan cheese

1. Place beef in a slow cooker, and season with salt and pepper. Add all remaining ingredients. Mix well.

2. Cover and cook on high for 3–4 hours or on low for 7–8 hours, until beef is fully cooked.

3. Remove and discard bay leaves.

MAKES 8 SERVINGS

228 calories

Prep: 10 minutes

Cook: 3–4 hours or 7–8 hours

You'll Need: slow cooker

⅛ of recipe (about 1 cup):
228 calories
6g total fat
(2g sat. fat)
585mg sodium
23.5g carbs
4g fiber
4g sugars
23.5g protein

italian wedding soup

Pictured on pages 48–49

Meatballs

1 pound raw extra-lean ground beef (at least 95% lean)
½ cup finely chopped onion
⅓ cup (about 3 large) egg whites or fat-free liquid egg substitute
1 teaspoon chopped garlic
1 teaspoon dried parsley
¼ teaspoon salt
¼ teaspoon black pepper

Soup

8 cups reduced-sodium chicken broth
2 cups chopped carrots
1 cup chopped celery
1 cup chopped onion
6 cups chopped spinach
2 cups frozen riced cauliflower

1. In a large bowl, combine all meatball ingredients. Evenly form into 30 meatballs, each about 1 inch in diameter.

2. Bring a skillet sprayed with nonstick spray to medium heat. Add meatballs, and cook until browned on all sides, about 6 minutes. Transfer meatballs to a slow cooker. Add broth, carrots, celery, and onion. Mix well.

3. Cover and cook on high for 3–4 hours or on low for 7–8 hours, until veggies are tender and meatballs are cooked through.

4. Turn off slow cooker. Add spinach and cauliflower. Mix well. Cover and let sit for 5–10 minutes, until cauliflower is hot and spinach has wilted.

MAKES 10 SERVINGS

108 calories

Prep: 20 minutes

Cook: 3–4 hours or 7–8 hours, plus 10 minutes

You'll Need: large bowl, skillet, nonstick spray, slow cooker

¹⁄₁₀ of recipe (about 1¼ cups):
108 calories
2.5g total fat
(1g sat. fat)
591mg sodium
8g carbs
2g fiber
3.5g sugars
13g protein

unstuffed cabbage soup

Pictured on pages 48–49

1¾ cups creamy tomato soup
12 ounces raw extra-lean ground beef (at least 95% lean)
1½ cups beef broth
1 cup chopped onion
½ cup jellied cranberry sauce
1½ tablespoons natural grape jelly
¼ teaspoon salt
¼ teaspoon black pepper
5 cups chopped cabbage (about ½ medium head)
Optional topping: chopped scallions

1. Spray a slow cooker with nonstick spray. Add all ingredients except cabbage. Mix well, using a spatula to break up the beef.

2. Cover and cook on high for 2 hours or on low for 4 hours.

3. Add cabbage. Cover and cook for 1 hour on high or 2 hours on low, until beef is cooked through and veggies are tender.

MAKES 5 SERVINGS

215 calories

Prep: 10 minutes

Cook: 3 hours or 6 hours

You'll Need: slow cooker, nonstick spray

⅕ **of recipe (about 1¼ cups):**
215 calories
4g total fat
(1.5g sat. fat)
675mg sodium
28.5g carbs
3g fiber
19.5g sugars
17.5g protein

hearty beef & potato soup

Pictured on pages 48–49

1 pound raw extra-lean ground beef (at least 95% lean)

1 teaspoon onion powder, divided

One 28-ounce can diced tomatoes (not drained)

3 cups beef broth

1½ cups chopped mushrooms

8 ounces (about 1 medium) russet potato, peeled and cubed

1 cup frozen sweet corn kernels

1 cup chopped onion

2 tablespoons tomato paste

1 tablespoon chopped garlic

1 teaspoon Italian seasoning

½ teaspoon ground thyme

1. Spray a slow cooker with nonstick spray. Add beef, and season with ½ teaspoon onion powder. Add all remaining ingredients, including remaining ½ teaspoon onion powder. Mix well, using a spatula to break up the beef.

2. Cover and cook on high for 3–4 hours or on low for 7–8 hours, until beef is fully cooked and veggies are tender.

MAKES 6 SERVINGS

208 calories

Prep: 10 minutes

Cook: 3–4 hours or 7–8 hours

You'll Need: slow cooker, nonstick spray

⅙ of recipe (about 1½ cups):
208 calories
3.5g total fat
(1.5g sat. fat)
654mg sodium
23g carbs
3g fiber
7.5g sugars
21g protein

Beef Barley Soup,
page 44

Italian
Wedding
Soup,
page 45

Split Pea Soup,
page 50

Unstuffed Cabbage
Soup, page 46

French Onion Soup,
page 51

Loaded Baked
Potato Soup,
page 52

Hearty Beef &
Potato Soup, page 47

split pea soup

Pictured on pages 48–49

4 cups chicken broth

2 cups dried split peas, rinsed

1½ cups chopped carrots

1½ cups chopped onion

8 ounces (about 1 medium) russet potato, peeled and cubed

6 ounces (about 9 slices) reduced-sodium ham, roughly chopped

1 tablespoon olive oil

2 teaspoons chopped garlic

1 teaspoon onion powder

2 bay leaves

¼ teaspoon ground thyme

¼ teaspoon salt

1. Add all ingredients to a slow cooker. Add 3 cups water. Mix well.

2. Cover and cook on high for 3–4 hours or on low for 7–8 hours, until veggies are tender.

3. Remove and discard bay leaves.

MAKES 8 SERVINGS

256 calories

 GF

Prep: 10 minutes

Cook: 3–4 hours or 7–8 hours

You'll Need: slow cooker

⅛ of recipe (about 1⅓ cups):
256 calories
3g total fat
(<0.5g sat. fat)
657mg sodium
42g carbs
14g fiber
7.5g sugars
17g protein

french onion soup

Pictured on pages 48–49

8 cups thinly sliced sweet onions
6 cups reduced-sodium beef broth
1½ tablespoons whipped butter
1 tablespoon balsamic vinegar
2 teaspoons chopped garlic
½ teaspoon salt
¼ teaspoon ground thyme
¼ teaspoon black pepper
4 slices whole-grain bread with 60–80 calories per slice
8 slices reduced-fat Swiss cheese

1. Add all ingredients except bread and cheese to a slow cooker. Lightly mix.

2. Cover and cook on high for 3–4 hours or low for 7–8 hours, until onions are tender and golden brown.

3. Meanwhile, toast the bread, and cut into quarters.

4. Portion soup into oven-safe bowls, and place bowls on a baking sheet. Top each bowl with 2 toast pieces and 1 slice of cheese. Broil until cheese has melted, about 3 minutes.

MAKES 8 SERVINGS

170 calories

Prep: 15 minutes

Cook: 3–4 hours or 7–8 hours, plus 5 minutes

You'll Need: slow cooker, 8 oven-safe bowls, baking sheet

⅛ of recipe (about 1 cup):
170 calories
6g total fat
(3g sat. fat)
619mg sodium
20g carbs
3g fiber
7g sugars
12.5g protein

loaded baked potato soup

Pictured on pages 48–49

6 cups (about 1 large) chopped cauliflower
3 cups chicken broth
14 ounces (about 2 medium) white potatoes, peeled and cubed
1 cup chopped onion
1 tablespoon chopped garlic
½ teaspoon salt
¼ teaspoon black pepper
2 cups fat-free milk
⅓ cup shredded reduced-fat cheddar cheese
4 slices center-cut bacon or turkey bacon
½ cup light sour cream
½ cup chopped scallions or chives

1. Place cauliflower, broth, potatoes, onion, garlic, salt, and pepper in a slow cooker. Mix well.

2. Cover and cook on high for 3–4 hours or on low for 7–8 hours, until veggies are tender.

3. Using a slotted spoon, transfer about half of the cooked veggies to a blender. Add milk, and puree until smooth.

4. Return pureed mixture to the slow cooker. Add cheese. Mix well. Cover and cook for 5 minutes, until soup is hot and cheese has melted.

5. Meanwhile, cook bacon until crispy, either in a skillet over medium heat or on a microwave-safe plate in the microwave. Chop or crumble.

6. Top each serving with 1 tablespoon sour cream, 1 tablespoon scallions, and about 1 tablespoon bacon.

MAKES 8 SERVINGS

149 calories

Prep: 15 minutes

Cook: 3–4 hours
or 7–8 hours, plus
5 minutes

You'll Need: slow
cooker, slotted spoon,
blender, skillet or
microwave-safe plate

⅛ of recipe
(about 1 cup):
149 calories
4g total fat
(2g sat. fat)
632mg sodium
20.5g carbs
3g fiber
8g sugars
8.5g protein

chicken sausage &
pepper stew

Pictured on pages 54–55

3 cups low-sodium chicken broth

2 cups chopped bell peppers

One 14.5-ounce can Italian-style stewed tomatoes (not drained)

12 ounces (about 3 medium) baby red potatoes, cubed

9 ounces (about 3 links) fully cooked chicken sausage, cut into coins

1 cup chopped onion

1 tablespoon chopped garlic

1 teaspoon Italian seasoning

1 teaspoon onion powder

3 cups roughly chopped spinach

1. Add all ingredients except spinach to a slow cooker. Mix well.

2. Cover and cook on high for 3–4 hours or on low for 7–8 hours, until potatoes and veggies are tender.

3. Add spinach. Stir until wilted.

MAKES 4 SERVINGS

243 calories

Prep: 15 minutes

Cook: 3–4 hours or 7–8 hours

You'll Need: slow cooker

¼ of recipe (about 2 cups):
243 calories
6g total fat
(1.5g sat. fat)
738mg sodium
32g carbs
5.5g fiber
11g sugars
17g protein

Chicken Sausage & Pepper Stew, page 53

Shrimp & Chicken Sausage Jambalaya, page 56

Tuscan Steak Stew,
page 57

Cajun Seafood
& Chicken
Sausage Stew,
page 58

shrimp & chicken sausage jambalaya

Pictured on pages 54–55

One 28-ounce can diced tomatoes (not drained)
2 cups chopped bell peppers
6 ounces (about 2 links) fully cooked chicken sausage, sliced into coins
1 tablespoon Cajun seasoning
1 bay leaf
4 cups frozen riced cauliflower
9 ounces (about 18) raw large shrimp, peeled, tails removed, deveined
¾ cup chopped fresh cilantro

1. Place tomatoes, peppers, and sausage in a slow cooker. Add Cajun seasoning and bay leaf, and mix well.

2. Cover and cook on high for 2½ hours or on low for 4½ hours.

3. Add cauliflower and shrimp. Mix well.

4. If cooking at low heat, increase to high. Cover and cook for 30 minutes, or until shrimp are cooked through.

5. Remove bay leaf. Serve topped with cilantro, 2 tablespoons per serving.

MAKES 6 SERVINGS

146 calories

Prep: 10 minutes

Cook: 2½ hours or 4½ hours, plus 30 minutes

You'll Need: slow cooker

⅙ of recipe (about 1¼ cups):
146 calories
3g total fat
(1g sat. fat)
679mg sodium
14.5g carbs
4.5g fiber
7.5g sugars
15.5g protein

tuscan steak stew

Pictured on pages 54–55

Two 14.5-ounce cans stewed tomatoes, lightly drained
⅓ cup balsamic vinegar
2 teaspoons garlic powder
1 teaspoon Italian seasoning
1¼ pounds raw lean steak, cut into bite-sized pieces
¼ teaspoon salt
¼ teaspoon black pepper
8 ounces green beans, trimmed
6 cups roughly chopped spinach

1. Add tomatoes, vinegar, garlic powder, and Italian seasoning to a slow cooker. Mix well.

2. Season steak with salt and pepper. Add steak and green beans. Mix well.

3. Cover and cook on high for 3–4 hours or on low for 7–8 hours, until steak is cooked through and green beans are tender.

4. Add spinach. Stir until wilted.

MAKES 4 SERVINGS

311 calories

Prep: 10 minutes

Cook: 3–4 hours or 7–8 hours

You'll Need: slow cooker

¼ of recipe (about 1½ cups):
311 calories
9g total fat
(3.5g sat. fat)
715mg sodium
21.5g carbs
4.5g fiber
12g sugars
34.5g protein

cajun seafood & chicken sausage stew

Pictured on pages 54–55

4 cups frozen diced potatoes

3 cups low-sodium chicken broth

One 14.5-ounce can fire-roasted diced tomatoes (not drained)

1½ cups chopped bell peppers

1½ cups chopped onion

12 ounces (about 4 links) fully cooked andouille-style chicken sausage, sliced into coins

1 cup chopped celery

1 tablespoon Cajun seasoning

1 tablespoon chopped garlic

10 ounces raw cod, cut into bite-sized pieces

8 ounces (about 24) raw medium shrimp, peeled, deveined, tails removed

½ cup light/reduced-fat cream cheese

1. Add all ingredients except cod, shrimp, and cream cheese to a slow cooker.

2. Cover and cook on high for 3–4 hours or on low for 7–8 hours, until veggies are tender.

3. If cooking at low heat, increase to high. Stir in cod and shrimp. Cover and cook for 30 minutes, or until cod and shrimp are fully cooked.

4. Add cream cheese. Mix until uniform.

MAKES 8 SERVINGS

248 calories

 GF

Prep: 15 minutes

Cook: 3–4 hours or 7–8 hours, plus 30 minutes

You'll Need: slow cooker

⅛ of recipe (about 1½ cups):
248 calories
7g total fat
(3g sat. fat)
667mg sodium
23g carbs
3g fiber
5.5g sugars
22.5g protein

HG FYI
This one has some heat! If you like things on the milder side, use less Cajun seasoning.

chilis

carne asada style chili

Pictured on pages 62–63

1 pound raw lean beef tenderloin roast, trimmed of excess fat
¼ teaspoon garlic powder
¼ teaspoon black pepper
One 29-ounce can tomato sauce
One 15-ounce can chili beans (pinto beans in chili sauce), not drained
One 15-ounce can red kidney beans, drained and rinsed
One 14.5-ounce can diced tomatoes, drained
2 cups chopped onion
1 cup chopped green bell pepper
2 tablespoons canned chipotle peppers in adobo sauce, chopped
2 teaspoons chopped garlic
1 teaspoon chili powder
1 teaspoon ground cumin
¼ cup chopped fresh cilantro
1 tablespoon lime juice

1. Spray a slow cooker with nonstick spray. Add beef, and season with garlic powder and black pepper.

2. Add remaining ingredients except cilantro and lime juice. Gently mix.

3. Cover and cook on high for 3–4 hours or on low for 7–8 hours, until beef is fully cooked and veggies are tender.

4. Remove beef, and cut into bite-sized pieces.

5. Return beef to the slow cooker. Add cilantro and lime juice. Mix well.

MAKES 9 SERVINGS

217 calories

Prep: 10 minutes

Cook: 3–4 hours or 7–8 hours

You'll Need: slow cooker, nonstick spray

⅑ of recipe (about 1 cup):
217 calories
4g total fat
(1g sat. fat)
834mg sodium
28g carbs
7.5g fiber
8.5g sugars
18g protein

white chicken chili bisque

Pictured on pages 62–63

1½ pounds raw extra-lean ground chicken (at least 98% lean)
¼ teaspoon salt
¼ teaspoon black pepper
3 cups reduced-sodium chicken broth
Two 15.5-ounce cans cannellini (white kidney) beans, drained
    and rinsed
1 cup chopped bell pepper
1 cup chopped onion
1 cup frozen sweet corn kernels
2 teaspoons chopped garlic
1 teaspoon chili powder
1 teaspoon ground cumin
¼ teaspoon cayenne pepper
½ cup instant mashed potato flakes
½ cup light/reduced-fat cream cheese

1. Spray a slow cooker with nonstick spray. Add chicken, and season with salt and black pepper. Add all remaining ingredients except potato flakes and cream cheese. Mix well, using a spatula to break up the chicken.

2. Cover and cook on high for 3–4 hours or on low for 7–8 hours, until chicken is fully cooked and veggies are tender.

3. Add potato flakes. Mix thoroughly. Add cream cheese. Mix until uniform.

MAKES 8 SERVINGS

279 calories

Prep: 10 minutes

Cook: 3–4 hours or
7–8 hours

You'll Need: slow cooker, nonstick spray

⅛ **of recipe**
(about 1¼ cups):
279 calories
4.5g total fat
(2g sat. fat)
581mg sodium
27.5g carbs
6g fiber
4g sugars
29.5g protein

jalapeño cheddar turkey chili

Pictured on pages 62–63

1 pound raw extra-lean ground turkey (at least 98% lean)

¼ teaspoon black pepper

One 28-ounce can crushed tomatoes

One 15-ounce can red kidney beans, drained and rinsed

1½ cups chopped brown mushrooms

1 cup chopped bell pepper

1 cup chopped onion

⅓ cup canned diced jalapeño peppers, drained

1 tablespoon chili seasoning

⅔ cup shredded reduced-fat cheddar cheese

1. Spray a slow cooker with nonstick spray. Add turkey, and season with pepper. Add remaining ingredients except cheese. Mix well, using a spatula to break up the turkey.

2. Cover and cook on high for 3–4 hours or on low for 7–8 hours, until turkey is fully cooked and veggies are tender.

3. Serve topped with cheese, about 2 tablespoons per serving.

MAKES 5 SERVINGS

304 calories

Prep: 10 minutes

Cook: 3–4 hours or 7–8 hours

You'll Need: slow cooker, nonstick spray

⅕ of recipe (about 1¼ cups): 304 calories 4.5g total fat (2g sat. fat) 894mg sodium 32.5g carbs 9.5g fiber 10g sugars 34g protein

HG Heads Up
Not all chili seasoning is gluten free. If you avoid gluten, check those labels.

Jalapeño Cheddar
Turkey Chili, page 61

White Chicken Chili Bisque, page 60

Autumn Veggie Chili, page 65

Carne Asada Style Chili, page 59

Best Beef & Bean Chili, page 64

best beef & bean chili

Pictured on pages 62–63

1 pound raw extra-lean ground beef (at least 95% lean)
¼ teaspoon salt
¼ teaspoon black pepper
One 15-ounce can red kidney beans, drained and rinsed
One 14.5-ounce can crushed tomatoes
One 14.5-ounce can diced tomatoes with green chiles (not drained)
1 cup chopped bell pepper
1 cup chopped onion
1 tablespoon chili seasoning

1. Spray a slow cooker with nonstick spray. Add beef, and season with salt and black pepper. Add remaining ingredients. Mix well, using a spatula to break up the beef.

2. Cover and cook on high for 3–4 hours or on low for 7–8 hours, until beef is fully cooked and veggies are tender.

MAKES 6 SERVINGS

214 calories

GF

Prep: 10 minutes

Cook: 3–4 hours or 7–8 hours

You'll Need: slow cooker, nonstick spray

⅙ of recipe (about 1 cup):
214 calories
3.5g total fat
(1.5g sat. fat)
736mg sodium
22.5g carbs
7g fiber
7.5g sugars
22g protein

HG Heads Up
Avoiding gluten? Check your chili seasoning! Some brands contain gluten.

autumn veggie chili

Pictured on pages 62–63

2½ cups canned crushed tomatoes

One 15-ounce can pure pumpkin

One 14.5-ounce can fire-roasted diced tomatoes (not drained)

2 teaspoons chopped garlic

1 tablespoon chili powder

1½ teaspoons ground cumin

1 teaspoon pumpkin pie spice

¼ teaspoon salt

4 cups cubed butternut squash

Two 15-ounce cans black beans, drained and rinsed

1 cup chopped red bell pepper

1 cup chopped red onion

¼ cup seeded and chopped jalapeño pepper

173 calories

Prep: 10 minutes

Cook: 3–4 hours or 7–8 hours

You'll Need: slow cooker, nonstick spray

⅑ of recipe (about 1 cup):
173 calories
0.5g total fat
(0g sat. fat)
539mg sodium
35g carbs
10g fiber
9g sugars
8g protein

1. Spray a slow cooker with nonstick spray. Add crushed tomatoes, pumpkin, fire-roasted tomatoes, garlic, and seasonings. Mix well. Add remaining ingredients. Gently stir.

2. Cover and cook on high for 3–4 hours or on low for 7–8 hours, until veggies have softened.

MAKES 9 SERVINGS

HG Tip
A medium butternut squash yields about 4 cups cubed squash. You can also find pre-cubed squash in the produce section!

DIY chili bar

Whether you're serving a crowd or a party of one, a solid stash of chili toppings is always a good idea! Here are some favorites . . .

reduced-fat shredded Mexican-blend cheese • light sour cream or fat-free plain Greek yogurt • fresh cilantro • avocado • jalapeño • crushed tortilla chips • scallions • red onion • tomato, salsa, or pico de gallo • hot sauce

apps & sides

homestyle mashies

Pictured on pages 68–69

3 cups cauliflower florets
12 ounces (about 9) baby red potatoes, halved
¼ cup light/reduced-fat cream cheese
¼ cup light sour cream
¾ teaspoon onion powder
½ teaspoon garlic powder
½ teaspoon salt
⅛ teaspoon black pepper
Optional topping: chopped scallions

1. Spray a slow cooker with nonstick spray. Add cauliflower, potatoes, and 1 cup water.

2. Cover and cook on high for 2–3 hours or on low for 5–6 hours, until cauliflower and potatoes are soft.

3. Turn off slow cooker. Drain cauliflower and potatoes. Transfer to a large bowl.

4. Add all remaining ingredients. Thoroughly mash and mix.

MAKES 5 SERVINGS

108 calories

Prep: 10 minutes

Cook: 2–3 hours or 5–6 hours

You'll Need: slow cooker, nonstick spray, colander, large bowl, potato masher

⅕ of recipe (about ⅔ cup):
108 calories
3.5g total fat
(2g sat. fat)
331mg sodium
16g carbs
2.5g fiber
4g sugars
4g protein

HG Alternative
Some like it skinless . . . Peel the potatoes first if that's how you like your mashed spuds.

ranch & bacon mashies

Pictured on pages 68–69

3 cups cauliflower florets
12 ounces (about 9) baby red potatoes, halved
¼ cup light/reduced-fat cream cheese
¼ cup light sour cream
2 teaspoons ranch dressing/dip seasoning mix
⅓ cup precooked crumbled bacon

1. Spray a slow cooker with nonstick spray. Add cauliflower, potatoes, and 1 cup water.

2. Cover and cook on high for 2–3 hours or on low for 5–6 hours, until potatoes and cauliflower are soft.

3. Turn off slow cooker. Drain potato and cauliflower. Transfer to a large bowl.

4. Add all remaining ingredients except bacon. Thoroughly mash and mix. Stir in bacon.

MAKES 5 SERVINGS

155 calories

Prep: 10 minutes

Cook: 2–3 hours or 5–6 hours

You'll Need: slow cooker, nonstick spray, colander, large bowl, potato masher

⅕ of recipe (about ⅔ cup):
155 calories
6g total fat
(3g sat. fat)
476mg sodium
17.5g carbs
2g fiber
3.5g sugars
8g protein

Homestyle Mashies,
page 66

Ranch & Bacon Mashies,
page 67

Classic Baked
Potatoes,
page 70

classic baked potatoes

Pictured on pages 68–69

Four 8-ounce russet potatoes
¼ teaspoon garlic powder
¼ teaspoon onion powder
¼ teaspoon salt
¼ teaspoon black pepper

1. Pierce potatoes several times with a fork. Place each potato on a piece of aluminum foil. Lightly spray with nonstick spray, and top with seasonings. Wrap foil around each potato, and place in a slow cooker.

2. Cover and cook on high for 3–4 hours or on low for 7–8 hours, until potatoes are tender.

MAKES 4 SERVINGS

178 calories

Prep: 5 minutes

Cook: 3–4 hours or 7–8 hours

You'll Need: aluminum foil, nonstick spray, slow cooker

¼ of recipe (1 potato):
178 calories
<0.5g total fat
(0g sat. fat)
156mg sodium
41g carbs
3g fiber
1.5g sugars
4.5g protein

baked potato bar

Now that you know the secret to perfectly slow-cooked potatoes, it's time to fill those taters with stuff . . .

crumbled bacon • chives • reduced-fat shredded cheddar cheese • light sour cream or fat-free plain Greek yogurt • tomato, salsa, or pico de gallo • extra-lean beef, turkey, or chicken • BBQ sauce • whipped butter • red onion

spinach artichoke dip

Pictured on pages 72–73

One 16-ounce package frozen chopped spinach
One 14-ounce can artichoke hearts, drained and chopped
One 8-ounce can sliced water chestnuts, drained and chopped
8 ounces light/reduced-fat cream cheese
1 cup part-skim shredded mozzarella cheese
¼ cup fat-free plain Greek yogurt
1½ tablespoons chopped garlic
½ teaspoon salt
2 tablespoons grated Parmesan cheese

1. Spray a slow cooker with nonstick spray. Add all ingredients except Parm. Mix well. Top with Parm.

2. Cover and cook on high for 3–4 hours or on low for 7–8 hours, until hot and bubbly.

MAKES 10 SERVINGS

131 calories

Prep: 10 minutes

Cook: 3–4 hours or 7–8 hours

You'll Need: slow cooker, nonstick spray

¹⁄₁₀ of recipe (about ⅓ cup):
131 calories
7g total fat
(4.5g sat. fat)
508mg sodium
8g carbs
2g fiber
2g sugars
8g protein

Buffalo Chicken Dip,
page 74

Taco Dip,
page 75

Spinach Artichoke Dip,
page 71

buffalo chicken dip

Pictured on pages 72–73

2½ cups frozen riced cauliflower
12 ounces cooked and shredded skinless chicken breasts
8 ounces light/reduced-fat cream cheese
½ cup Frank's RedHot Original Cayenne Pepper Sauce
½ cup shredded part-skim mozzarella cheese
¼ cup fat-free plain Greek yogurt
¼ cup light ranch dressing
Optional topping: fresh chives

1. Spray a slow cooker with nonstick spray. Add all ingredients. Mix well.

2. Cover and cook on high for 1 hour or on low for 3 hours, until hot and thickened.

MAKES 12 SERVINGS

126 calories

Prep: 5 minutes

Cook: 1 hour or 3 hours

You'll Need: slow cooker, nonstick spray

¹⁄₁₂ of recipe (about ⅓ cup):
126 calories
7g total fat
(3.5g sat. fat)
574mg sodium
3.5g carbs
0.5g fiber
2g sugars
12g protein

dip it good

What's a dip without its dippers? Mix and match . . .

Fresh Veggies: Baby carrots and celery sticks are classic go-tos, but don't sleep on jicama sticks, mini bell peppers, sliced cucumber, and sugar snap peas!

Crunchy Snacks: There are so many better-for-you crisps on supermarket shelves! Reach for baked tortilla chips, whole-grain crackers, popped chips, and puffed snacks.

taco dip

Pictured on pages 72–73

Two 16-ounce cans fat-free refried beans
1 pound raw extra-lean ground beef (at least 95% lean)
2 cups chopped tomatoes
1 cup finely chopped onion
Two 4-ounce cans diced green chiles
1½ teaspoons taco seasoning
½ cup shredded reduced-fat Mexican-blend cheese

1. Spray a slow cooker with nonstick spray. Add all ingredients except cheese. Mix well, using a spatula to break up the beef.

2. Cover and cook on high for 3–4 hours or on low for 7–8 hours, until beef is fully cooked.

3. Turn off slow cooker. Stir in cheese.

4. Let sit, uncovered, until slightly thickened, 10–15 minutes.

MAKES 12 SERVINGS

149 calories

GF

Prep: 10 minutes

Cook: 3–4 hours or 7–8 hours

Cool: 15 minutes

You'll Need: slow cooker, nonstick spray

**¹⁄₁₂ of recipe
(about ½ cup):**
149 calories
2.5g total fat
(1g sat. fat)
478mg sodium
17g carbs
5g fiber
2g sugars
14g protein

HG Tip
If you follow a gluten-free diet, check the ingredients on your taco seasoning. (Some have it, some don't.)

low & slow ratatouille

Pictured on pages 78–79

4 cups cubed eggplant

2 cups roughly chopped red bell peppers

2 cups sliced and halved zucchini

One 14.5-ounce can fire-roasted diced tomatoes (not drained)

1 cup roughly chopped onion

½ cup tomato paste

1 teaspoon garlic powder

1 teaspoon onion powder

½ teaspoon dried oregano

½ teaspoon salt

¼ teaspoon black pepper

⅓ cup chopped fresh basil

1. Spray a slow cooker with nonstick spray. Add all ingredients except basil. Mix well.

2. Cover and cook on high for 3–4 hours or on low for 7–8 hours, until veggies have softened.

3. Stir in basil.

MAKES 6 SERVINGS

80 calories

Prep: 15 minutes

Cook: 3–4 hours or 7–8 hours

You'll Need: slow cooker, nonstick spray

⅙ of recipe (about 1 cup):
80 calories
0.5g total fat
(0g sat. fat)
380mg sodium
17g carbs
5g fiber
10g sugars
3.5g protein

chunky root veggie hash

Pictured on pages 78–79

2 cups cubed butternut squash

1¼ cups vegetable broth

8 ounces (about 1 medium) russet potato, peeled and cubed

1 cup chopped carrots

1 cup chopped celery

1 cup chopped onion

2 tablespoons chopped garlic

1 tablespoon finely chopped fresh sage

1 teaspoon finely chopped fresh thyme

1 bay leaf

½ teaspoon salt

½ teaspoon black pepper

2 cups chopped kale

Optional topping: Parmesan cheese

1. Spray a slow cooker with nonstick spray. Add all ingredients except kale. Mix well.

2. Cover and cook on high for 3–4 hours or on low for 7–8 hours, until veggies have softened.

3. Remove and discard bay leaf. Stir in kale. Cover and cook until kale has wilted, about 20 minutes.

MAKES 6 SERVINGS

87 calories

Prep: 10 minutes

Cook: 3–4 hours or 7–8 hours, plus 20 minutes

You'll Need: slow cooker

⅙ of recipe (about 1 cup):
87 calories
<0.5g total fat
(0g sat. fat)
409mg sodium
20g carbs
3g fiber
4.5g sugars
2.5g protein

Chunky Root Veggie
Hash, page 77

Veggie-Boosted
Rice & Beans,
page 81

Low & Slow Ratatouille, page 76

Cinnamon Applesauce, page 82

Cranberry Balsamic Brussels Sprouts, page 80

cranberry balsamic brussels sprouts

Pictured on pages 78–79

1 tablespoon Dijon mustard
1 tablespoon olive oil
½ teaspoon salt
⅛ teaspoon black pepper
1 pound Brussels sprouts, trimmed and halved
⅓ cup sweetened dried cranberries, chopped
½ cup balsamic vinegar

1. In a medium bowl, combine mustard, oil, salt, pepper, and ¼ cup water. Whisk thoroughly.

2. Spray a slow cooker with nonstick spray. Add Brussels sprouts, cranberries, and mustard mixture. Stir to coat.

3. Cook on high for 1½ hours or on low for 3½ hours, or until sprouts are tender and lightly browned.

4. Bring vinegar to a boil in a small nonstick pot. Reduce to a simmer. Stirring frequently, cook until thickened to a syrup-like consistency, about 12 minutes.

5. Drizzle Brussels sprouts with balsamic reduction.

MAKES 4 SERVINGS

138 calories

Prep: 10 minutes

Cook: 1½ hours or 3½ hours, plus 15 minutes

You'll Need: medium bowl, whisk, slow cooker, nonstick spray, small nonstick pot

¼ of recipe (about ¾ cup):
138 calories
3.5g total fat
(0.5g sat. fat)
398mg sodium
23.5g carbs
5g fiber
14g sugars
3.5g protein

veggie-boosted rice & beans

Pictured on pages 78–79

Two 15-ounce cans red kidney beans, drained and rinsed
1½ cups chopped bell pepper
1½ cups chopped onion
2 cups vegetable broth
½ cup uncooked brown rice
1 tablespoon chopped garlic
1 bay leaf
½ teaspoon salt
½ teaspoon onion powder
¼ teaspoon cayenne pepper
¼ teaspoon ground thyme
1½ cups frozen riced cauliflower

1. Spray a slow cooker with nonstick spray. Add all ingredients except cauliflower.

2. Cover and cook on high for 3–4 hours or low for 7–8 hours, until veggies are tender and rice is fully cooked.

3. Turn off slow cooker. Remove and discard bay leaf.

4. Add cauliflower. Mix well. Cover and let sit for 5–10 minutes, until hot.

MAKES 6 SERVINGS

214 calories

Prep: 10 minutes

Cook: 3–4 hours or 7–8 hours, plus 10 minutes

You'll Need: slow cooker, nonstick spray

⅙ of recipe (about 1 cup):
214 calories
1g total fat
(0g sat. fat)
697mg sodium
42g carbs
9.5g fiber
6.5g sugars
10.5g protein

cinnamon applesauce

Pictured on pages 78–79

4 cups peeled and sliced Fuji apples
4 cups peeled and sliced Granny Smith apples
2 tablespoons cornstarch
¼ cup natural no-calorie sweetener that measures like sugar
2 teaspoons cinnamon
2 teaspoons lemon juice
1 teaspoon vanilla extract
¼ teaspoon salt
⅛ teaspoon ground nutmeg

1. Spray a slow cooker with nonstick spray. Add apples.

2. In a medium bowl, combine cornstarch with ¾ cup water. Whisk to dissolve. Add remaining ingredients. Whisk well.

3. Pour cornstarch mixture over apples. Stir to coat.

4. Cover and cook on high for 2½ hours or on low for 4½ hours, until apples have completely softened and liquid has thickened.

5. Thoroughly mash and mix.

MAKES 8 SERVINGS

64 calories

Prep: 10 minutes

Cook: 2½ hours or 4½ hours

You'll Need: slow cooker, nonstick spray, medium bowl, whisk, potato masher

⅛ of recipe (about ½ cup):
64 calories
<0.5g total fat
(0g sat. fat)
73mg sodium
22.5g carbs
1.5g fiber
11g sugars
<0.5g protein

meal starters

shredded orange sesame chicken

Pictured on pages 86–87

½ cup chicken broth
⅓ cup orange marmalade
2 tablespoons reduced-sodium soy sauce
2 teaspoons chopped garlic
1 teaspoon onion powder
1½ pounds raw boneless skinless chicken breasts
¼ teaspoon salt
¼ teaspoon black pepper
1 tablespoon sesame seeds
Optional seasoning: red pepper flakes

1. Spray a slow cooker with nonstick spray. Add broth, marmalade, soy sauce, garlic, and onion powder. Stir until uniform.

2. Season chicken with salt and pepper, and add it to the slow cooker.

3. Cover and cook on high for 3–4 hours or on low for 7–8 hours, until chicken is fully cooked.

4. Transfer chicken to a large bowl. Shred with two forks.

5. Return chicken to slow cooker. Add sesame seeds, and mix well.

MAKES 6 SERVINGS

195 calories

Prep: 10 minutes

Cook: 3–4 hours or 7–8 hours

You'll Need: slow cooker, nonstick spray, large bowl

⅙ **of recipe
(about ½ cup):**
195 calories
3.5g total fat
(0.5g sat. fat)
397mg sodium
13g carbs
0.5g fiber
10g sugars
26.5g protein

shredded honey BBQ chicken

Pictured on pages 86–87

¾ cup **BBQ sauce**

¼ cup **honey**

½ teaspoon **garlic powder**

½ teaspoon **onion powder**

1½ pounds **raw boneless skinless chicken breasts**

¼ teaspoon **salt**

¼ teaspoon **black pepper**

1 cup **chopped red onion**

1. Spray a slow cooker with nonstick spray. Add BBQ sauce, honey, garlic powder, and onion powder. Mix until uniform.

2. Season chicken with salt and pepper, and add it to the slow cooker. Top with onion.

3. Cover and cook on high for 3–4 hours or on low for 7–8 hours, until chicken is fully cooked and onion is tender.

4. Transfer chicken to a bowl, and shred with two forks.

5. Return chicken to the slow cooker. Mix well.

MAKES 6 SERVINGS

246 calories

Prep: 10 minutes

Cook: 2–3 hours or 5–6 hours, plus 10 minutes

You'll Need: slow cooker, nonstick spray, large bowl

⅙ of recipe (about ⅔ cup):
246 calories
3g total fat
(0.5g sat. fat)
439mg sodium
28g carbs
0.5g fiber
24.5g sugars
26g protein

chipotle lime beef barbacoa

Pictured on pages 86–87

3 pounds raw boneless chuck beef roast, trimmed of excess fat,
   cut into large pieces
¾ teaspoon salt, divided
¼ teaspoon black pepper
One 10-ounce can diced tomatoes with green chiles (not drained)
1 cup chopped onion
½ cup beef broth
2 tablespoons apple cider vinegar
2 tablespoons chopped canned chipotle peppers
1½ tablespoons lime juice
1 tablespoon canned adobo sauce
1 tablespoon chopped garlic
1½ teaspoons ground cumin
½ teaspoon dried oregano
¼ teaspoon cayenne pepper
1 bay leaf
Optional toppings: fresh cilantro, chopped scallions

173 calories

 GF

Prep: 15 minutes

Cook: 3–4 hours or
7–8 hours

You'll Need: slow
cooker, nonstick spray,
large bowl

**¹⁄₁₂ of recipe
(about ½ cup):**
173 calories
7g total fat
(3g sat. fat)
375mg sodium
3g carbs
0.5g fiber
1.5g sugars
24.5g protein

1. Spray a slow cooker with nonstick spray. Add beef, and season with ½ teaspoon salt and black pepper. Add remaining ingredients, including the remaining ¼ teaspoon salt. Mix well.

2. Cook on high for 3–4 hours or on low for 7–8 hours, until beef is fully cooked.

3. Remove and discard bay leaf. Transfer beef to a large bowl. Shred with two forks.

4. Return beef to the slow cooker. Mix well.

MAKES 12 SERVINGS

HG Tip
Look for chipotle peppers packed in
adobo sauce in the Mexican food aisle.
Two ingredients in one!

Shredded Salsa Verde Chicken, page 89

Cranberry Pulled Pork, page 88

Shredded Honey BBQ Chicken, page 84

Beef Ragu,
page 90

Shredded Orange
Sesame Chicken,
page 83

Chipotle
Lime Beef
Barbacoa,
page 85

cranberry pulled pork

Pictured on pages 86–87

¼ cup spicy brown mustard
½ teaspoon garlic powder
12 ounces raw lean boneless pork tenderloin, trimmed of excess fat
12 ounces raw boneless pork shoulder, trimmed of excess fat
¼ teaspoon salt
¼ teaspoon black pepper
2 cups roughly chopped onion
1 cup sweetened dried cranberries

1. In a small bowl, combine mustard, garlic powder, and 2 teaspoons water. Mix well.

2. Spray a slow cooker with nonstick spray. Add both kinds of pork to the slow cooker, and season with salt and pepper.

3. Top with onion, cranberries, and mustard mixture.

4. Cover and cook on high for 3–4 hours or on low for 7–8 hours, until pork is fully cooked.

5. Transfer pork to a large bowl. Shred with two forks.

6. Return shredded pork to the slow cooker. Mix well.

MAKES 6 SERVINGS

234 calories

Prep: 20 minutes

Cook: 3–4 hours or 7–8 hours

You'll Need: small bowl, slow cooker, nonstick spray, large bowl

⅙ of recipe (about ⅔ cup):
234 calories
4.5g total fat
(1.5g sat. fat)
287mg sodium
23g carbs
2g fiber
17g sugars
23g protein

shredded salsa verde chicken

Pictured on pages 86–87

1 pound raw boneless skinless chicken breasts
¼ teaspoon salt
¼ teaspoon black pepper
1 cup salsa verde (tomatillo salsa)
½ cup chopped green bell pepper
½ cup chopped onion
One 4-ounce can diced green chiles (not drained)
1½ teaspoons chopped garlic
½ teaspoon ground cumin
½ teaspoon chili powder
Optional topping: fresh cilantro

1. Spray a slow cooker with nonstick spray. Add chicken, and season with salt and black pepper. Add ½ cup water and all remaining ingredients. Mix well.

2. Cover and cook on high for 3–4 hours or on low for 7–8 hours, until chicken is fully cooked.

3. Transfer chicken to a large bowl. Shred with two forks.

4. Return chicken to the slow cooker, and mix well.

MAKES 4 SERVINGS

187 calories

GF

Prep: 10 minutes

Cook: 3–4 hours or 7–8 hours

You'll Need: slow cooker, nonstick spray, large bowl

¼ of recipe (about 1 cup):
187 calories
3.5g total fat
(0.5g sat. fat)
749mg sodium
10.5g carbs
1.5g fiber
4g sugars
26g protein

beef ragu

Pictured on pages 86–87

One 28-ounce can crushed tomatoes
½ cup beef broth
½ cup dry red wine
¼ cup tomato paste
2 bay leaves
1 teaspoon Italian seasoning
1 packet natural no-calorie sweetener
1 cup finely chopped mushrooms
1 cup finely chopped onion
2 pounds raw boneless chuck beef roast, trimmed of excess fat and cut
  into large pieces
1 teaspoon garlic powder
½ teaspoon salt
¼ teaspoon black pepper

1. Spray a slow cooker with nonstick spray. Add tomatoes, broth, wine, tomato paste, bay leaves, Italian seasoning, and sweetener. Mix well.

2. Stir in mushrooms and onion.

3. Season beef with garlic powder, salt, and pepper. Add it to the slow cooker.

4. Cover and cook on high for 3–4 hours or on low for 7–8 hours, until beef is fully cooked and veggies are tender.

5. Remove and discard bay leaves. Transfer beef to a large bowl. Shred with two forks.

6. Return beef to the slow cooker. Mix well.

MAKES 6 SERVINGS

302 calories

 GF

Prep: 10 minutes

Cook: 3–4 hours or 7–8 hours

You'll Need: slow cooker, nonstick spray, large bowl

⅙ of recipe (1 heaping cup):
302 calories
9g total fat
(4g sat. fat)
678mg sodium
16.5g carbs
4g fiber
7g sugars
35.5g protein

make it a meal!

They're called meal starters for a reason! Serve up these recipes in the following ways . . .

in taco shells • wrapped in a tortilla • in lettuce cups • over shredded lettuce • over riced cauliflower and/or brown rice • over zucchini noodles and/or whole-grain pasta • in a baked potato • in steamed cabbage leaves • in bell pepper halves

Shredded Orange Sesame Chicken, page 83

scoopable beef burritos

1½ pounds raw boneless chuck beef roast, trimmed of excess fat
and cut into large pieces
½ teaspoon salt, divided
¼ teaspoon black pepper
One 15-ounce can black beans, drained and rinsed
One 14.5-ounce can diced tomatoes, drained
1 cup chopped onion
One 4-ounce can diced green chiles, drained
1½ cups reduced-sodium beef broth
1 tablespoon chili powder
1 tablespoon ground cumin
½ teaspoon garlic powder
½ teaspoon onion powder
½ teaspoon paprika
5 cups frozen riced cauliflower
½ cup shredded reduced-fat Mexican-blend cheese
Optional seasonings: additional salt and black pepper

1. Spray a slow cooker with nonstick spray. Add beef, and season
with ¼ teaspoon salt and pepper. Top with beans, tomatoes,
onion, and green chiles.

2. Add broth and seasonings, including remaining ¼ teaspoon
salt. Gently stir.

3. Cover and cook on high for 3–4 hours or on low for 7–8 hours,
until beef is fully cooked.

4. Turn off slow cooker. Transfer beef to a large bowl. Shred with
two forks.

5. Return beef to the slow cooker. Add cauliflower. Mix well. Cover
and let sit for 5–10 minutes, until hot.

6. Serve with a slotted spoon, draining the liquid. Top each
serving with 1 tablespoon cheese.

MAKES 8 SERVINGS

395 calories

Prep: 15 minutes

Cook: 3–4 hours
or 7–8 hours, plus
10 minutes

You'll Need: slow
cooker, nonstick spray,
large bowl, slotted
spoon

**⅛ of recipe
(about 1 cup):**
395 calories
14.5g total fat
(6g sat. fat)
751mg sodium
19g carbs
5.5g fiber
5g sugars
50g protein

garlic parm chicken

1½ pounds raw boneless skinless chicken breasts
¼ teaspoon salt
¼ teaspoon black pepper
1½ cups chicken broth
1 cup chopped onion
1 tablespoon chopped garlic
½ cup light/reduced-fat cream cheese
¼ cup grated Parmesan cheese
½ teaspoon garlic powder
½ teaspoon onion powder

1. Spray a slow cooker with nonstick spray. Add chicken, and season with salt and pepper. Add broth, onion, and garlic.

2. Cover and cook on high for 3–4 hours or on low for 7–8 hours, until chicken is fully cooked.

3. Meanwhile, place cream cheese in a large bowl. Stir until smooth. Add Parm, garlic powder, and onion powder. Mix until uniform.

4. Transfer chicken to a cutting board, and roughly chop. Add to the large bowl.

5. Using a slotted spoon, transfer onion to the bowl. Mix well.

MAKES 6 SERVINGS

224 calories

 GF

Prep: 10 minutes

Cook: 3–4 hours or 7–8 hours

You'll Need: slow cooker, nonstick spray, large bowl, slotted spoon

⅙ of recipe (about ¾ cup):
224 calories
8.5g total fat
(4g sat. fat)
535mg sodium
5g carbs
0.5g fiber
2.5g sugars
30g protein

HG Tip
Save the leftover cooking broth for another time . . . It's delicious as a soup starter!

beef stroganoff

1½ tablespoons au jus gravy mix
1 pound raw lean beef tenderloin roast, trimmed of excess fat
¼ teaspoon salt
¼ teaspoon black pepper
3 cups sliced mushrooms
1½ cups chopped onion
2 tablespoons cornstarch
½ cup light/reduced-fat cream cheese
1 pound (about 2 medium) spiralized zucchini

1. Spray a slow cooker with nonstick spray. Add gravy mix and ⅓ cup water. Stir to dissolve.

2. Season beef with salt and pepper, and add it to the slow cooker. Top with mushrooms and onion. Cover and cook on high for 3–4 hours or on low for 7–8 hours, until beef is fully cooked.

3. Transfer beef to a large bowl. Shred (or roughly chop).

4. If cooking at low heat, increase to high. In a small bowl, combine cornstarch with 2 tablespoons water. Stir to dissolve. Stir into the liquid in the slow cooker. Add cream cheese, and mix until uniform.

5. Return beef to the slow cooker. Mix well. Stir in zucchini.

6. Cover and cook for 20 minutes, or until zucchini is hot and slightly softened.

MAKES 4 SERVINGS

320 calories

GF

Prep: 10 minutes

Cook: 3–4 hours or 7–8 hours, plus 20 minutes

You'll Need: slow cooker, nonstick spray, large bowl, small bowl

¼ of recipe (about 1 cup):
320 calories
14.5g total fat
(6.5g sat. fat)
745mg sodium
18.5g carbs
3g fiber
7.5g sugars
30.5g protein

HG Heads Up
If you avoid gluten, check the ingredients on your gravy mix to make sure it's gluten free.

casseroles

classic chicken pot pie

Pictured on opposite page

1 pound raw boneless skinless chicken breasts,
    cut into bite-sized pieces
¼ teaspoon salt
¼ teaspoon black pepper
3 cups frozen petite mixed vegetables
Two 10.5-ounce cans (about 2½ cups) organic cream of mushroom
    condensed soup
1½ teaspoons poultry seasoning
1 teaspoon chopped garlic
1 package refrigerated organic crescent dough

1. Spray a slow cooker with nonstick spray. Add chicken, and season with salt and pepper. Add remaining ingredients except dough. Mix well.

2. Roll out dough into a shape and size similar to your slow cooker opening, and smooth out the perforations. Place it over the contents of the slow cooker.

3. Cover and cook on high for 2–3 hours or on low for 5–6 hours.

4. If cooking at low heat, increase to high. Vent lid. Cook until chicken is cooked through and top is golden brown, about 30 minutes.

5. Turn off slow cooker. Remove lid, and let sit for 10 minutes.

MAKES 6 SERVINGS

320 calories

Prep: 10 minutes

Cook: 2–3 hours or 5–6 hours, plus 30 minutes

Cool: 10 minutes

You'll Need: slow cooker, nonstick spray

⅙ of recipe:
320 calories
11g total fat
(4.5g sat. fat)
890mg sodium
30g carbs
2g fiber
5.5g sugars
20.5g protein

dough-topped tip

To reheat a recipe that's topped with crescent dough, here's how to keep it crisp. Pop a serving into an oven-safe dish, and crank up the oven to 400°F. In 8–10 minutes, you'll have a hot entrée with a well-done topper!

Classic
Chicken
Pot Pie,
opposite
page

Hungry Duke
Casserole,
page 100

hungry duke casserole

Pictured on page 99

This is my take on the famous John Wayne casserole . . . A beefy, cheesy masterpiece!

1 pound raw extra-lean ground beef (at least 95% lean)
1½ tablespoons taco seasoning, divided
¼ cup light mayonnaise
¼ cup light sour cream
¾ cup shredded reduced-fat cheddar cheese, divided
1 cup chopped onion, divided
1 cup chopped mushrooms
¼ teaspoon garlic powder
1 cup chopped green bell pepper
1 cup sliced tomato
¼ cup canned sliced jalapeño peppers, drained
1 package refrigerated organic crescent dough

1. Bring a skillet sprayed with nonstick spray to medium-high heat. Add beef and 1 tablespoon taco seasoning. Cook, stir, and crumble until fully cooked, about 5 minutes.

2. In a medium bowl, mix mayo with sour cream. Add ½ cup cheddar cheese and ½ cup onion. Mix well.

3. Spray a slow cooker with nonstick spray. Add beef, mushrooms, garlic powder, and remaining ½ tablespoon taco seasoning. Mix well.

4. Evenly top with bell pepper, tomato, remaining ½ cup onion, jalapeño, and mayo mixture. Top with remaining ¼ cup cheddar cheese.

5. Roll out dough into a shape and size similar to your slow cooker opening, and smooth out the perforations. Place it over the contents of the slow cooker.

6. Cover and cook on high for 2–3 hours or on low for 5–6 hours.

7. If cooking at low heat, increase to high. Vent lid. Cook until beef is cooked through and top is golden brown, about 30 minutes.

8. Turn off slow cooker. Remove lid, and let sit for 10 minutes.

MAKES 6 SERVINGS

348 calories

Prep: 15 minutes

Cook: 2–3 hours or 5–6 hours, plus 35 minutes

Cool: 10 minutes

You'll Need: skillet, nonstick spray, slow cooker

⅙ of recipe:
348 calories
16g total fat
(6.5g sat. fat)
777mg sodium
25.5g carbs
1.5g fiber
7g sugars
22.5g protein

Another Dough-Topped Tip
Drape a layer of paper towels over the slow cooker before adding the lid, and use the lid to secure it. This will absorb moisture and help the topping to brown!

shepherd's pie

Pictured on page 102

1 pound raw extra-lean ground beef (at least 95% lean)

1 cup chopped onion

1 teaspoon chopped garlic

¼ teaspoon plus ⅛ teaspoon salt, divided

¼ teaspoon plus ⅛ teaspoon black pepper, divided

3 cups frozen petite mixed vegetables, thawed and drained

One 10.5-ounce can (about 1¼ cups) organic cream of mushroom condensed soup

1 cup instant mashed potato flakes

3 cups frozen cauliflower florets

2 tablespoons light/reduced-fat cream cheese

⅛ teaspoon garlic powder

⅛ teaspoon onion powder

1. Spray a slow cooker with nonstick spray.

2. Bring a skillet sprayed with nonstick spray to medium-high heat. Add beef, onion, garlic, ¼ teaspoon salt, and ¼ teaspoon pepper. Cook, stir, and crumble until beef is fully cooked and onion has softened, 5–7 minutes.

3. Spray a slow cooker with nonstick spray. Add beef mixture, mixed veggies, and soup. Mix well.

4. Cover and cook on high for 3–4 hours or on low for 7–8 hours.

5. In a large microwave-safe bowl, combine potato flakes with 1½ cups hot water. Mix well. Stir in cauliflower. Cover and microwave for 3 minutes, or until potatoes have thickened and cauliflower is hot. Thoroughly mash. Add cream cheese, garlic powder, onion powder, remaining ⅛ teaspoon salt, and remaining ⅛ teaspoon pepper. Mix well.

6. If cooking at low heat, increase to high. Spoon potato topping over the filling, and smooth out the surface. Cover and cook until hot, about 20 minutes.

MAKES 4 SERVINGS

355 calories

Prep: 15 minutes

Cook: 2–3 hours or 5–6 hours, plus 30 minutes

You'll Need: skillet, nonstick spray, slow cooker, large microwave-safe bowl, potato masher

¼ of recipe:
355 calories
9g total fat
(4g sat. fat)
680mg sodium
36.5g carbs
6g fiber
8g sugars
30.5g protein

BBQ Chicken Cornbread Casserole, opposite page

Black Bean & Beef Tamale Pie, page 104

Shepherd's Pie, page 101

BBQ chicken cornbread casserole

Pictured on opposite page

1 pound raw boneless skinless chicken breasts, cut into bite-sized pieces
1 cup BBQ sauce
1 cup chopped bell pepper
1 cup frozen sweet corn kernels
1 cup chopped onion
½ cup all-purpose flour
⅓ cup yellow cornmeal
2 tablespoons natural no-calorie sweetener that measures like sugar
1½ teaspoon baking powder
⅛ teaspoon salt
¾ cup canned cream-style corn
⅓ cup (about 3 large) egg whites or fat-free liquid egg substitute
⅓ cup fat-free plain Greek yogurt, or more for topping
Optional toppings: chopped scallions, cilantro

301 calories

Prep: 15 minutes

Cook: 2–3 hours or 6–7 hours, plus 1 hour

You'll Need: slow cooker, nonstick spray, large bowl

⅙ of recipe:
301 calories
3g total fat
(0.5g sat. fat)
715mg sodium
49.5g carbs
2g fiber
21.5g sugars
23.5g protein

1. Spray a slow cooker with nonstick spray. Add chicken, BBQ sauce, pepper, frozen corn, and onion. Mix well, and smooth out the top.

2. Cover and cook on high for 2–3 hours or on low for 6–7 hours.

3. In a large bowl, combine flour, cornmeal, sweetener, baking powder, and salt. Mix well. Add cream-style corn, egg whites/substitute, and yogurt. Mix until uniform. Pour mixture over the contents of the slow cooker, and smooth out the top.

4. If cooking at low heat, increase to high. Cover and cook for 1 hour, until chicken is fully cooked and cornbread has set.

MAKES 6 SERVINGS

black bean & beef tamale pie

Pictured on page 102

1 pound raw extra-lean ground beef (at least 95% lean)
1½ tablespoons taco seasoning, divided
1 cup beef broth
¾ cup yellow cornmeal
2 tablespoons natural no-calorie sweetener that measures like sugar
¼ teaspoon salt, divided
One 14.5-ounce can diced tomatoes with chiles (not drained)
1½ cups chopped onion
¾ cup frozen sweet corn kernels
½ cup canned black beans, drained and rinsed
Optional toppings: shredded reduced-fat cheddar cheese, light sour
    cream, sliced black olives

1. Bring a skillet sprayed with nonstick spray to medium-high heat. Add beef and 1 tablespoon taco seasoning. Cook, stir, and crumble until fully cooked, about 5 minutes.

2. In a medium bowl, mix broth, cornmeal, sweetener, and ⅛ teaspoon salt. Let stand for 5 minutes.

3. Spray a slow cooker with nonstick spray. Add beef and remaining ingredients, including remaining ½ tablespoon taco seasoning and ⅛ teaspoon salt. Mix well.

4. Top with cornmeal mixture.

5. Cover and cook on high for 3–4 hours or on high for 7–8 hours on low, until veggies are tender and topping has set.

MAKES 6 SERVINGS

225 calories

 GF

Prep: 15 minutes

Cook: 5 minutes, plus 3–4 hours or 7–8 hours

Cool: 5 minutes

You'll Need: skillet, nonstick spray, medium bowl, slow cooker

⅙ of recipe:
225 calories
4g total fat
(1.5g sat. fat)
665mg sodium
30.5g carbs
4g fiber
4.5g sugars
20g protein

HG Heads Up
Some taco seasoning contains gluten, so read labels carefully if you avoid it.

scoopable classic lasagna

Pictured on page 12

1 pound raw extra-lean ground beef (at least 95% lean)

2½ cups marinara sauce with 70 calories or less per ½-cup serving, divided

½ cup chopped onion

1 teaspoon chopped garlic

One 15-ounce container (about 2 cups) low-fat cottage cheese

1½ cups shredded part-skim mozzarella cheese

¼ cup (about 2 large) egg whites or fat-free liquid egg substitute

4 ounces (about 4½) uncooked whole-grain lasagna noodles, broken into pieces, divided

One 10-ounce package frozen chopped spinach, thawed and drained, divided

382 calories

Prep: 15 minutes

Cook: 5 minutes, plus 3–4 hours or 7–8 hours

You'll Need: skillet, nonstick spray, large bowl, medium bowl, slow cooker

⅙ of recipe:
382 calories
11.5g total fat
(5.5g sat. fat)
878mg sodium
30.5g carbs
4.5g fiber
10g sugars
38.5g protein

1. Bring a skillet sprayed with nonstick spray to medium-high heat. Add beef. Cook, stir, and crumble until fully cooked, about 5 minutes. Transfer to a large bowl. Add ½ cup marinara sauce, onion, and garlic. Mix thoroughly.

2. In a medium bowl, combine cottage cheese, mozzarella, and egg whites/substitute. Mix well.

3. Spray a slow cooker with nonstick spray. Spread 1 cup marinara sauce along the bottom. Top with 2 ounces noodles, half of the beef mixture, half of the thawed and drained spinach, and half of the cheese mixture. Continue layering with ½ cup marinara sauce and remaining noodles, beef mixture, spinach, and cheese. Spread remaining ½ cup marinara sauce over the top.

4. Cover and cook on high for 3–4 hours or on low for 7–8 hours, until pasta is fully cooked and the top has lightly browned.

MAKES 6 SERVINGS

veggie enchilada casserole

One 15-ounce can black beans, drained and rinsed
1 cup frozen sweet corn kernels
1 cup chopped onion
1 cup chopped zucchini
One 4-ounce can chopped green chiles
2 cups canned red enchilada sauce, divided
Six 6-inch corn tortillas, divided
1½ cups shredded reduced-fat Mexican-blend cheese, divided
Optional toppings: sliced avocado, light sour cream, cilantro

1. In a large bowl, combine black beans, corn, onion, zucchini, chiles, and ½ cup enchilada sauce. Mix well.

2. Spray a slow cooker with nonstick spray. Spread ½ cup enchilada sauce along the bottom, and top with two tortillas, side by side.

3. Evenly spoon half of the bean mixture over the tortillas. Top with ½ cup cheese. Repeat layering with 2 tortillas, ½ cup enchilada sauce, remaining bean mixture, ½ cup cheese, remaining 2 tortillas, remaining ½ cup enchilada sauce, and remaining ½ cup cheese.

4. Cover and cook on high for 3–4 hours or on low for 7–8 hours, until veggies are tender and casserole has set.

MAKES 6 SERVINGS

257 calories

Prep: 15 minutes

Cook: 3–4 hours or 7–8 hours

You'll Need: large bowl, slow cooker, nonstick spray

⅙ of recipe:
257 calories
8g total fat
(3.5g sat. fat)
892mg sodium
35g carbs
5.5g fiber
5g sugars
13.5g protein

turkey sausage and stuffing casserole

One 12-ounce jar turkey (or chicken) gravy
1 cup chopped celery
1 cup chopped mushrooms
1 cup chopped onion
One 6-ounce box turkey stuffing mix
⅓ cup sweetened dried cranberries, chopped
2 tablespoons whipped butter
1 pound raw extra-lean ground turkey (at least 98% lean)
¼ teaspoon ground sage
¼ teaspoon ground thyme
¼ teaspoon salt
¼ teaspoon black pepper
⅛ teaspoon ground nutmeg

268 calories

Prep: 10 minutes

Cook: 3–4 hours or 7–8 hours

You'll Need: slow cooker, nonstick spray, large bowl

⅙ of recipe:
268 calories
5.5g total fat
(1g sat. fat)
770mg sodium
31.5g carbs
2.5g fiber
8g sugars
22.5g protein

1. Spray a slow cooker with nonstick spray. Add gravy, veggies, stuffing mix, cranberries, and butter. Mix well.

2. In a large bowl, season turkey with seasonings. Mix thoroughly. Spoon mixture over the contents of the slow cooker.

3. Cover and cook on high for 3–4 hours or on low for 7–8 hours, until turkey is cooked through.

MAKES 6 SERVINGS

 *pasta*

classic macaroni & cheese

Pictured on pages 112–113

5 cups chopped cauliflower
½ cup fat-free milk
5 ounces (about 1½ cups) uncooked whole-grain elbow macaroni
½ cup shredded reduced-fat cheddar cheese, or more for topping
½ cup whipped cream cheese
¼ cup light sour cream
1 teaspoon garlic powder
½ teaspoon onion powder
½ teaspoon salt
¼ teaspoon black pepper
Optional: grated Parmesan cheese

1. Spray a slow cooker with nonstick spray. Add cauliflower, milk, and 2 cups water.

2. Cover and cook on high for 2–3 hours or on low for 5–6 hours, until cauliflower is tender.

3. If cooking at low heat, increase to high. Stir in macaroni. Cover and cook for 10 minutes, or until pasta is al dente, stirring halfway through.

4. Turn off slow cooker. Add remaining ingredients. Mix until uniform.

MAKES 4 SERVINGS

282 calories

Prep: 10 minutes

Cook: 2–3 hours or 5–6 hours, plus 10 minutes

You'll Need: slow cooker, nonstick spray

¼ of recipe (about 1 cup):
282 calories
9.5g total fat
(5.5g sat. fat)
559mg sodium
38.5g carbs
6g fiber
8.5g sugars
13.5g protein

jalapeño popper mac & cheese

Pictured on pages 112–113

5 cups chopped cauliflower

½ cup fat-free milk

5 ounces (about 1½ cups) uncooked whole-grain elbow macaroni

One 4-ounce can diced jalapeños, drained

½ cup shredded part-skim mozzarella cheese

½ cup whipped cream cheese

¼ cup light sour cream

1 teaspoon garlic powder

½ teaspoon onion powder

¼ teaspoon salt

¼ teaspoon black pepper

Optional toppings: grated Parmesan cheese, toasted panko bread crumbs

1. Spray a slow cooker with nonstick spray. Add cauliflower, milk, and 2 cups water.

2. Cover and cook on high for 2–3 hours or on low for 5–6 hours, until cauliflower is tender.

3. If cooking at low heat, increase to high. Stir in macaroni. Cover and cook for 10 minutes, or until pasta is al dente, stirring halfway through.

4. Turn off slow cooker. Add remaining ingredients. Mix until uniform.

MAKES 4 SERVINGS

285 calories

Prep: 10 minutes

Cook: 2–3 hours or 5–6 hours, plus 10 minutes

You'll Need: slow cooker, nonstick spray

¼ of recipe (about 1 cup):
285 calories
9.5g fat
(5.5g sat. fat)
543mg sodium
39.5g carbs
6g fiber
8.5g sugars
14g protein

Jalapeño Popper
Mac & Cheese,
page 111

Pizza Macaroni & Cheese,
page 114

Classic Macaroni
& Cheese,
page 110

pizza macaroni & cheese

Pictured on pages 112–113

2 cups canned crushed tomatoes
1 teaspoon garlic powder
1 teaspoon onion powder
½ teaspoon Italian seasoning
¼ teaspoon salt
5 cups chopped cauliflower
5 ounces (about 1½ cups) uncooked whole-grain elbow macaroni
½ cup shredded part-skim mozzarella cheese
½ cup whipped cream cheese
1½ ounces (about 22 pieces) turkey pepperoni, chopped, divided
Optional topping: grated Parmesan cheese

317 calories

Prep: 10 minutes

Cook: 2–3 hours
or 5–6 hours, plus
10 minutes

You'll Need: slow
cooker, nonstick spray

**¼ of recipe
(about 1¼ cups):**
317 calories
9.5g total fat
(5g sat. fat)
839mg sodium
44g carbs
8.5g fiber
9.5g sugars
17g protein

1. Spray a slow cooker with nonstick spray. Add tomatoes, seasonings, and 1 cup water. Mix until uniform. Stir in cauliflower.

2. Cover and cook on high for 2–3 hours or on low for 5–6 hours, until cauliflower is tender.

3. Stir in macaroni. Cover and cook for 10 minutes, or until pasta is al dente, stirring halfway through.

4. Turn off slow cooker. Add mozzarella, cream cheese, and half of the pepperoni. Mix until uniform.

5. Serve topped with remaining pepperoni.

MAKES 4 SERVINGS

butternut squash & sage pasta

Pictured on pages 116–117

3 cups cubed butternut squash

1 cup chopped apple

1 cup chopped onion

5 ounces (about 1½ cups) uncooked whole-grain penne or rigatoni pasta

¼ cup whipped butter

2 tablespoons brown sugar

1 teaspoon garlic powder

½ teaspoon salt

¼ teaspoon black pepper

¼ teaspoon ground sage

Optional topping: grated Parmesan cheese

1. Spray a slow cooker with nonstick spray. Add squash, apple, and onion. Top with 1½ cups water.

2. Cover and cook on high for 2–3 hours or on low for 5–6 hours, or until veggies and apple are tender.

3. If cooking at low heat, increase to high. Stir in pasta. Cover and cook for 25 minutes, or until pasta is al dente, stirring halfway through.

4. Turn off slow cooker. Add remaining ingredients. Mix until uniform.

MAKES 4 SERVINGS

281 calories

Prep: 10 minutes

Cook: 2–3 hours or 5–6 hours, plus 25 minutes

You'll Need: slow cooker, nonstick spray

¼ of recipe (about 1 cup):
281 calories
7.5g total fat
(3.5g sat. fat)
352mg sodium
51.5g carbs
6.5g fiber
13.5g sugars
6g protein

Penne Marinara with
Meat Sauce, page 119

Cheesy
Hamburger
Noodles,
page 118

Butternut
Squash &
Sage Pasta,
page 115

cheesy hamburger noodles

Pictured on pages 116–117

Just like my mom made—only healthier!

1 pound raw extra-lean ground beef (at least 95% lean)
½ teaspoon garlic powder
½ teaspoon onion powder
3 cups chopped cauliflower
Two 10.5-ounce cans (about 2½ cups) organic cream of mushroom condensed soup
2 cups chopped onion
½ cup finely chopped celery
5 ounces (about 1½ cups) uncooked whole-grain penne or rigatoni pasta
1 cup shredded reduced-fat cheddar cheese, or more for topping

1. Spray a slow cooker with nonstick spray. Add beef, and season with garlic powder and onion powder. Add cauliflower, soup, onion, and celery. Mix well, using a spatula to break up the beef.

2. Cover and cook on high for 3–4 hours or on low for 7–8 hours.

3. Stir in pasta. Cover and cook for 25 minutes, or until pasta is al dente, stirring halfway through.

4. Turn off slow cooker. Add cheese. Mix until uniform.

MAKES 6 SERVINGS

335 calories

Prep: 10 minutes

Cook: 3–4 hours or 7–8 hours, plus 25 minutes

You'll Need: slow cooker, nonstick spray

⅙ of recipe (about 1 cup):
335 calories
11g total fat
(5g sat. fat)
584mg sodium
33.5g carbs
5g fiber
6g sugars
26.5g protein

---

be a pasta pro!

These recipes call for whole-grain pasta—like whole wheat—because it's high in fiber and satisfying. Other great noodle options are lentil pasta, bean pasta, and edamame pasta. (Just keep an eye on them as cook time may vary.)

Nobody likes mushy pasta, so here's a tip: If you're not eating a pasta-based slow-cooker recipe right away, transfer it to a large serving bowl or into containers immediately. That'll prevent it from continuing to cook from the heat of the slow cooker.

penne marinara with meat sauce

Pictured on pages 116–117

1 pound raw extra-lean ground beef (at least 95% lean)
¼ teaspoon salt
¼ teaspoon black pepper
3 cups marinara sauce with 70 calories or less per ½-cup serving
1½ cups chopped mushrooms
1 cup chopped tomatoes
1 tablespoon chopped garlic
1 teaspoon Italian seasoning
½ teaspoon onion powder
5 ounces (about 1½ cups) uncooked whole-grain penne pasta
1 cup frozen peas
½ cup whipped cream cheese
2 tablespoons grated Parmesan cheese

319 calories

Prep: 10 minutes

Cook: 3–4 hours or 7–8 hours, plus 25 minutes

You'll Need: slow cooker, nonstick spray

⅙ of recipe (about 1 cup):
319 calories
9g total fat
(3.5g sat. fat)
781mg sodium
35g carbs
6g fiber
11g sugars
25g protein

1. Spray a slow cooker with nonstick spray. Add beef, and season with salt and pepper. Add marinara sauce, mushrooms, tomatoes, garlic, Italian seasoning, onion powder, and 1½ cups water. Mix well, using a spatula to break up the beef.

2. Cover and cook on high for 3–4 hours or on low for 7–8 hours, until beef is fully cooked.

3. If cooking at low heat, increase to high. Stir in pasta. Cover and cook for 20 minutes, or until pasta is almost al dente, stirring halfway through.

4. Turn off slow cooker. Add peas and cream cheese. Mix until uniform.

5. Cover and let sit for 5 minutes, or until entire dish is hot.

6. Serve topped with Parm, 1 teaspoon per serving.

MAKES 6 SERVINGS

garlic brown sugar chicken thighs

Pictured on pages 122–123

Five 4½-ounce raw boneless skinless chicken thighs
½ teaspoon onion powder
½ teaspoon salt
¼ teaspoon black pepper
1 cup chopped onion
⅓ cup brown sugar
1½ tablespoon chopped garlic

1. Spray a slow cooker with nonstick spray. Add chicken, and season with onion powder, salt, and pepper. Top with onion, brown sugar, and garlic.

2. Cover and cook on high for 2–3 hours or on low for 5–6 hours, until chicken is fully cooked and onion is tender.

MAKES 5 SERVINGS

207 calories

Prep: 5 minutes

Cook: 2–3 hours or 5–6 hours

You'll Need: slow cooker, nonstick spray

⅕ of recipe (1 thigh with onion):
207 calories
5g total fat
(1.5g sat. fat)
358mg sodium
14g carbs
0.5g fiber
10.5g sugars
25g protein

creamy mushroom chicken thighs

Pictured on pages 122–123

**One 10.5-ounce can (about 1¼ cups) organic cream of
mushroom condensed soup**
1 cup chicken broth
½ teaspoon ground thyme
Five 4½-ounce raw boneless skinless chicken thighs
¼ teaspoon salt
¼ teaspoon black pepper
2 cups sliced mushrooms

1. Spray a slow cooker with nonstick spray. Add soup, broth, and thyme. Mix well.

2. Season chicken with salt and pepper, and add it to the slow cooker. Top with mushrooms.

3. Cover and cook on high for 2–3 hours or on low for 5–6 hours, until chicken is fully cooked and mushrooms are tender.

MAKES 5 SERVINGS

197 calories

Prep: 5 minutes

Cook: 2–3 hours or
5–6 hours

You'll Need: slow
cooker, nonstick spray

**⅕ of recipe
(1 thigh with sauce):**
197 calories
7g total fat
(2g sat. fat)
619mg sodium
5.5g carbs
1g fiber
1g sugars
26.5g protein

Garlic Brown Sugar
Chicken Thighs,
page 120

Creamy Mushroom
Chicken Thighs,
page 121

Teriyaki Chicken
Thighs, page 124

Garlic Brown Sugar
Chicken Thighs,
page 120

teriyaki chicken thighs

Pictured on pages 122–123

½ cup canned crushed pineapple in juice (not drained)
½ cup thick teriyaki sauce or marinade, or more for topping
2 teaspoons chopped garlic
½ teaspoon ground ginger
Five 4½-ounce raw boneless skinless chicken thighs
⅛ teaspoon salt
⅛ teaspoon black pepper
1 cup chopped onion
Optional toppings: chopped scallions, sesame seeds

1. Spray a slow cooker with nonstick spray. Add pineapple, teriyaki sauce, garlic, and ginger. Mix well.

2. Season chicken with salt and pepper, and add to the slow cooker. Top with onion.

3. Cover and cook on high for 2–3 hours or on low for 5–6 hours, until chicken is fully cooked and onion is tender.

MAKES 5 SERVINGS

218 calories

Prep: 5 minutes

Cook: 2–3 hours or 5–6 hours

You'll Need: slow cooker, nonstick spray

**⅕ of recipe
(1 thigh with sauce):**
218 calories
5.5g total fat
(1.5g sat. fat)
831mg sodium
15g carbs
1g fiber
10g carbs
25.5g protein

fall-apart pork tenderloin

Pictured on pages 128–129

1 pound raw pork tenderloin, trimmed of excess fat
2 tablespoons chopped garlic
1½ tablespoons olive oil
½ teaspoon Italian seasoning
½ teaspoon ground thyme
½ teaspoon salt
⅛ teaspoon black pepper
⅛ teaspoon dried sage

1. Spray a slow cooker with nonstick spray. Add pork.

2. In a small bowl, combine garlic, oil, and seasonings. Mix well. Rub mixture over the pork.

3. Cover and cook on high for 3–4 hours or on low for 7–8 hours, until pork is cooked through.

MAKES 4 SERVINGS

189 calories

Prep: 5 minutes

Cook: 3–4 hours or 7–8 hours

You'll Need: slow cooker, nonstick spray, small bowl

¼ of recipe:
189 calories
8.5g total fat
(1.5g sat. fat)
357mg sodium
1.5g carbs
<0.5g fiber
0g sugars
24g protein

maple glazed pork tenderloin

Pictured on pages 128–129

1 pound raw pork tenderloin, trimmed of excess fat
1½ teaspoons garlic powder
½ teaspoon salt
⅛ teaspoon black pepper
1½ tablespoons natural sugar-free pancake syrup
1 tablespoon brown mustard
2 cups (about 2 medium) sliced pears
1½ cups chopped onion
1 tablespoon chopped chives

1. Spray a slow cooker with nonstick spray. Add pork, and season with garlic powder, salt, and pepper.

2. In a large bowl, combine syrup and mustard. Mix well. Add pears and onion, and toss to coat. Add to the slow cooker.

3. Cover and cook on high for 3–4 hours or on low for 7–8 hours, until pork is cooked through and pears and onion are tender.

4. Top with chives.

MAKES 4 SERVINGS

209 calories

Prep: 10 minutes

Cook: 3–4 hours or 7–8 hours

You'll Need: slow cooker, nonstick spray, large bowl

¼ of recipe:
209 calories
3.5g total fat
(1g sat. fat)
447mg sodium
17.5g carbs
3g fiber
9.5g sugars
24.5g protein

smothered pork tenderloin & onions

Pictured on pages 128–129

1½ tablespoons au jus gravy mix
1 pound raw pork tenderloin, trimmed of excess fat
½ teaspoon garlic powder
¼ teaspoon ground thyme
⅛ teaspoon salt
⅛ teaspoon black pepper
4 cups sliced onions
1 tablespoon cornstarch
½ cup light/reduced-fat cream cheese

1. Spray a slow cooker with nonstick spray. Add gravy mix and ⅓ cup water. Stir to dissolve.

2. Season pork with garlic powder, thyme, salt, and pepper. Add to the slow cooker. Top with onions.

3. Cover and cook on high for 3–4 hours or on low for 7–8 hours, until pork is fully cooked.

4. Transfer pork to a cutting board. Slice pork.

5. In a small bowl, combine cornstarch with 1 tablespoon water. Stir to dissolve. Stir mixture into the liquid in the slow cooker.

6. Add cream cheese, and mix until uniform.

7. Return sliced pork to the slow cooker, and gently stir to coat.

MAKES 4 SERVINGS

272 calories

Prep: 10 minutes

Cook: 3–4 hours or 7–8 hours

You'll Need: slow cooker, nonstick spray, small bowl

¼ of recipe:
272 calories
9.5g total fat
(4.5g sat. fat)
679mg sodium
17g carbs
2g fiber
6g sugars
23.5g protein

HG Heads Up
Some gravy mix contains gluten, so read labels carefully if that's a concern.

Smothered Pork
Tenderloin & Onions,
page 127

Fall-Apart Pork
Tenderloin,
page 125

Garlic Brown
Sugar Pork
Tenderloin,
page 130

Maple Glazed Pork
Tenderloin, page 126

garlic brown sugar pork tenderloin

Pictured on pages 128–129

1 pound raw pork tenderloin, trimmed of excess fat
2 tablespoons brown sugar
1 tablespoon chopped garlic
1 tablespoon olive oil
½ teaspoon salt
¼ teaspoon black pepper
⅛ teaspoon smoked paprika
1½ cups chopped onion
1 cup carrots cut into coins

1. Spray a slow cooker with nonstick spray. Add pork.

2. In a small bowl, combine brown sugar, garlic, oil, and seasonings. Mix well. Rub mixture over the pork. Top with onion and carrots.

3. Cover and cook on high for 3–4 hours or on low for 7–8 hours, until pork is cooked through and veggies have softened.

MAKES 4 SERVINGS

208 calories

Prep: 10 minutes

Cook: 3–4 hours or 7–8 hours

You'll Need: slow cooker, nonstick spray, small bowl

¼ of recipe:
208 calories
6g total fat
(1.5g sat. fat)
381mg sodium
14g carbs
2g fiber
8.5g sugars
24g protein

beer braised chicken

Pictured on pages 134–135

1½ pounds raw boneless skinless chicken breasts,
   cut into 2-inch chunks
¾ teaspoon salt
½ teaspoon garlic powder
¼ teaspoon smoked paprika
1 cup chopped carrots
1 cup chopped onion
10 ounces (about 3) small baby red potatoes, cubed
¾ cup Guinness beer (or another dark beer)
1 tablespoon brown sugar

1. Spray a slow cooker with nonstick spray. Add chicken, and season with seasonings. Add remaining ingredients and ⅓ cup water. Mix well.

2. Cover and cook on high for 3–4 hours or on low for 7–8 hours, until chicken is cooked through and veggies are tender.

3. Serve with a slotted spoon, draining the liquid.

MAKES 6 SERVINGS

218 calories

Prep: 10 minutes

Cook: 3–4 hours or 7–8 hours

You'll Need: slow cooker, nonstick spray, slotted spoon

⅙ of recipe (about ¾ cup):
218 calories
3g total fat
(0.5g sat. fat)
360mg sodium
16.5g carbs
2g fiber
3.5g sugars
27g protein

herb chicken with root veggies

Pictured on pages 134–135

Four 4-ounce raw boneless skinless chicken breast cutlets
¾ teaspoon salt, divided
½ teaspoon black pepper, divided
2 cups onion cut into 1-inch chunks
1 cup peeled carrots cut into 1-inch chunks
1 cup peeled parsnip cut into 1-inch chunks
1 cup peeled beets cut into 1-inch chunks
1 cup reduced-sodium chicken broth
2 tablespoons whipped butter, melted
2 tablespoons chopped fresh basil
2 tablespoons chopped garlic
2 tablespoons chopped fresh oregano

1. Spray a slow cooker with nonstick spray. Add chicken, and season with ½ teaspoon salt and ¼ teaspoon pepper. Top with veggies, and season with remaining ¼ teaspoon salt and ¼ teaspoon pepper. Add broth.

2. In a small bowl, combine melted butter, basil, garlic, and oregano. Mix well. Top veggies with butter mixture.

3. Cover and cook on high for 3–4 hours or on low for 7–8 hours, until chicken is cooked through and veggies have softened.

MAKES 4 SERVINGS

273 calories

Prep: 15 minutes

Cook: 3–4 hours or 7–8 hours

You'll Need: slow cooker, nonstick spray, small bowl

**¼ of recipe
(1 cutlet with about
1 cup veggies):**
273 calories
6.5g total fat
(2.5g sat. fat)
714mg sodium
24.5g carbs
6g fiber
11g sugars
28.5g protein

floosh's pineapple chicken

Pictured on pages 134–135

This is my version of a yummy dish my mom made at least twice a month when I was growing up!

1 pound raw boneless skinless chicken breasts
½ **teaspoon salt**
¼ **teaspoon black pepper**
Two 14.5-ounce cans stewed tomatoes (not drained)
1½ **cups chopped green bell pepper**
1½ **cups chopped onion**
One 8-ounce can pineapple chunks packed in juice (not drained)
Optional topping: fresh chives

1. Spray a slow cooker with nonstick spray. Add chicken, and season with salt and black pepper. Add remaining ingredients. Mix well.

2. Cover and cook on high for 3–4 hours or on low for 7–8 hours, until chicken is fully cooked.

3. Transfer chicken to a cutting board. Roughly chop.

4. Return chopped chicken to the slow cooker. Mix well.

MAKES 6 SERVINGS

174 calories

Prep: 5 minutes

Cook: 3–4 hours or 7–8 hours

You'll Need: slow cooker, nonstick spray

⅙ **of recipe (about 1 cup):**
174 calories
2g total fat
(0.5g sat. fat)
534mg sodium
19g carbs
3g fiber
13g sugars
19g protein

Floosh's Pineapple Chicken, page 133

Herb Chicken with Root Veggies, page 132

Beer Braised Chicken,
page 131

Chicken and Scalloped
Potatoes, page 136

chicken and scalloped potatoes

Pictured on pages 134–135

12 ounces (about 1 medium) russet potato
12 ounces (about 1 medium) turnip
1 cup light sour cream
¼ cup reduced-fat shredded cheddar cheese
¼ cup light/reduced-fat cream cheese
¼ cup fat-free milk
1 tablespoon chopped garlic
½ teaspoon salt
¼ teaspoon black pepper
1 pound raw boneless skinless chicken breasts, cut into
    bite-sized pieces
¼ cup chopped scallions, or more for topping

1. Spray a slow cooker with nonstick spray.

2. Peel potatoes and turnip. Thinly slice into half-moon slices.

3. In a large bowl, combine all remaining ingredients except chicken and scallions. Mix until uniform.

4. Add chicken and scallions to the large bowl. Mix well.

5. Place ⅓ of the potato and turnip slices in an even layer along the bottom. Top with ⅓ of the chicken mixture. Repeat layering twice with remaining potato and turnip slices and chicken mixture.

6. Cover and cook on high for 3–4 hours or on low for 7–8 hours, until chicken is fully cooked and potatoes and turnips are tender.

7. Turn off slow cooker. Remove lid. Let sit until slightly thickened, about 15 minutes.

MAKES 4 SERVINGS

370 calories

Prep: 10 minutes

Cook: 3–4 hours or 7–8 hours

Cool: 15 minutes

You'll Need: vegetable peeler, large bowl, slow cooker, nonstick spray

¼ of recipe (about 1 cup):
370 calories
12.5g total fat
(6g sat. fat)
599mg sodium
28.5g carbs
3g fiber
11.5g sugars
34.5g protein

the memphis philly

Pictured on page 138

1 cup canned crushed tomatoes
½ cup ketchup
2½ tablespoons brown sugar
2½ tablespoons apple cider vinegar
2 teaspoons garlic powder
12 ounces raw boneless pork shoulder, trimmed of excess fat
12 ounces raw lean boneless pork tenderloin, trimmed of excess fat
⅛ teaspoon salt
⅛ teaspoon black pepper
2 cups sliced green bell peppers
2 cups sliced onion
8 standard-sized hot dog buns (about 130 calories each)
4 slices reduced-fat provolone cheese, cut into thin strips

1. Spray a slow cooker with nonstick spray. Add crushed tomatoes, ketchup, brown sugar, vinegar, and garlic powder. Mix well.

2. Season both types of pork with salt and black pepper. Add pork to the slow cooker. Top with bell peppers and onion.

3. Cover and cook on high for 3–4 hours or on low for 7–8 hours, until pork is cooked through and veggies are tender.

4. Transfer cooked peppers and onion to a medium bowl.

5. Transfer pork to a large bowl. Shred with two forks. Return shredded pork to the slow cooker. Mix well.

6. Preheat oven to 425°F. Spray a baking sheet with nonstick spray.

7. Place hot dog buns on the baking sheet, split sides up. Bake until lightly toasted, about 2 minutes.

8. Using a slotted spoon to drain excess liquid, evenly distribute pork among the hot dog buns, about ½ cup each. Top with veggies, about ¼ cup each. Top with cheese.

9. Bake sandwiches until cheese has melted, about 4 minutes.

MAKES 8 SERVINGS

323 calories

Prep: 20 minutes

Cook: 3–4 hours or 7–8 hours, plus 10 minutes

You'll Need: slow cooker, nonstick spray, medium bowl, large bowl, baking sheet, slotted spoon

⅛ of recipe (1 sandwich):
323 calories
7g total fat
(2.5g sat. fat)
622mg sodium
38.5g carbs
3.5g fiber
13.5g sugars
26g protein

Sloppy Jane
Stuffed
Peppers,
opposite page

The Memphis Philly,
page 137

sloppy jane stuffed peppers

Pictured on opposite page

4 large bell peppers
1¼ cups canned crushed tomatoes
2 tablespoons tomato paste
1 tablespoon honey
1 tablespoon dried minced onion
1 tablespoon red wine vinegar
1 tablespoon Worcestershire sauce
1 teaspoon molasses
¾ teaspoon salt
¼ teaspoon black pepper
1 pound raw extra-lean ground turkey (at least 98% lean)
2 cups frozen riced cauliflower, thawed and drained
Optional topping: shredded reduced-fat cheddar cheese

1. Spray a slow cooker with nonstick spray.

2. Carefully slice off and discard stem ends of bell peppers. Remove and discard seeds.

3. In a large bowl, combine tomatoes, tomato paste, honey, dried onion, vinegar, Worcestershire sauce, molasses, salt, and black pepper. Mix until smooth and uniform. Stir in turkey and cauliflower.

4. Distribute mixture among the peppers. Place peppers in the slow cooker.

5. Cover and cook on high for 2–3 hours or on low for 5–6 hours, until turkey is fully cooked and peppers are tender.

MAKES 4 SERVINGS

234 calories

 GF

Prep: 10 minutes

Cook: 2–3 hours or 5–6 hours

You'll Need: slow cooker, large bowl

¼ of recipe (1 stuffed pepper):
234 calories
2g total fat
(<0.5g sat. fat)
418mg sodium
25.5g carbs
6.5g fiber
16g sugars
31.5g protein

HG Tip
Look for bell peppers that sit flat when stem ends are up.

scoopable thanksgiving supper

Pictured on opposite page

1½ pounds raw boneless skinless turkey breast cutlets
1¼ teaspoons poultry seasoning, divided
¾ teaspoon salt, divided
¼ teaspoon black pepper
½ cup chicken broth
12 slices whole-grain bread with 60–80 calories per slice, cubed
1 cup chopped Granny Smith apple
1 cup chopped onion
½ cup chopped celery
⅓ cup sweetened dried cranberries
Optional topping: fat-free chicken or turkey gravy

1. Spray a slow cooker with nonstick spray. Add turkey, and season with ¼ teaspoon poultry seasoning, ¼ teaspoon salt, and pepper. Top with broth.

2. In a large bowl, combine bread, apple, onion, celery, and cranberries. Add remaining 1 teaspoon poultry seasoning and ½ teaspoon salt. Mix until uniform. Add mixture to the slow cooker, gently pressing it over the top of turkey.

3. Cover and cook on high for 3–4 hours or on low for 7–8 hours, until turkey is cooked through and veggies and apple are tender.

MAKES 6 SERVINGS

312 calories

Prep: 10 minutes

Cook: 3–4 hours or 7–8 hours

You'll Need: slow cooker, nonstick spray, large bowl

⅙ of recipe (about 1 cup):
312 calories
3.5g total fat
(<0.5g sat. fat)
706mg sodium
39g carbs
6.5g fiber
12g sugars
33g protein

Classic Pot Roast,
page 150

Scoopable
Thanksgiving
Supper,
opposite page

garlic & herb steak and potatoes

1½ pounds raw lean steak, cut into bite-sized pieces
1 tablespoon chopped garlic
½ teaspoon salt
¼ teaspoon black pepper
1 pound (about 2 medium) russet potatoes, cubed
One 14.5-ounce can diced tomatoes (not drained)
8 ounces green beans, cut into ½-inch pieces
1 cup chopped onion
4 fresh thyme sprigs

1. Spray a slow cooker with nonstick spray. Add steak, and season with garlic, salt, and pepper. Add remaining ingredients. Mix well.

2. Cover and cook on high for 3–4 hours or on low for 7–8 hours, until steak is cooked through and veggies are tender.

3. Remove and discard thyme sprigs.

MAKES 6 SERVINGS

265 calories

Prep: 10 minutes

Cook: 3–4 hours or 7–8 hours

You'll Need: slow cooker, nonstick spray

⅙ **of recipe (about 1 cup):**
265 calories
7g total fat
(3g sat. fat)
381mg sodium
21.5g carbs
4g fiber
4g sugars
27.5g protein

EZ eggplant parm

6 cups cubed eggplant

2 cups chopped onion

2 cups cherry tomatoes

One 14.5-ounce can crushed tomatoes

1 cup chopped red bell pepper

½ cup tomato paste

2 tablespoons olive oil

1 tablespoon chopped garlic

2 teaspoons Italian seasoning

½ teaspoon salt

¼ teaspoon black pepper

⅓ cup chopped fresh basil, or more for topping

¼ cup grated Parmesan cheese

1 cup shredded part-skim mozzarella cheese

1. Spray a slow cooker with nonstick spray. Add all ingredients except basil, Parm, and mozzarella. Mix well.

2. Cover and cook on high for 3–4 hours or on low for 7–8 hours, until veggies are tender.

3. Turn off slow cooker. Stir in basil and Parm. Top with mozzarella. Cover and let sit for 5 minutes, or until mozzarella has melted.

MAKES 4 SERVINGS

339 calories

Prep: 15 minutes

Cook: 3–4 hours or 7–8 hours, plus 5 minutes

You'll Need: slow cooker, nonstick spray

¼ of recipe:
339 calories
15g total fat
(6g sat. fat)
890mg sodium
34.5g carbs
10.5g fiber
18.5g sugars
18g protein

saucy italian meatballs

2 cups marinara sauce with 70 calories or less per ½-cup serving
1 pound raw extra-lean ground beef (at least 95% lean)
1 cup finely chopped onion
⅓ cup (about 3 large) egg whites or fat-free liquid egg substitute
¼ cup panko bread crumbs
1 tablespoon grated Parmesan cheese, or more for topping
½ teaspoon garlic powder
½ teaspoon Italian seasoning
¼ teaspoon salt
¼ teaspoon black pepper
Serving suggestions: whole-grain pasta, spiralized zucchini

1. Spray a slow cooker with nonstick spray. Add marinara sauce.

2. In a large bowl, combine remaining ingredients. Thoroughly mix. Firmly and evenly form into 20 meatballs, and place them in the slow cooker.

3. Cover and cook on high for 3–4 hours or on low for 7–8 hours, until meatballs are fully cooked.

MAKES 5 SERVINGS

210 calories

Prep: 20 minutes

Cook: 3–4 hours or 7–8 hours

You'll Need: slow cooker, nonstick spray, large bowl

⅕ of recipe (4 meatballs with sauce):
210 calories
6g total fat
(2g sat. fat)
562mg sodium
15g carbs
2.5g fiber
7.5g sugars
23.5g protein

homestyle meatloaf

1 pound raw extra-lean ground beef (at least 95% lean)
1 cup finely chopped mushrooms
1 cup finely chopped onion
½ cup (about 4 large) egg whites or fat-free liquid egg substitute
½ cup panko bread crumbs
½ cup ketchup, divided
1 teaspoon garlic powder
1 teaspoon onion powder
¼ teaspoon salt
¼ teaspoon black pepper

200 calories

Prep: 10 minutes

Cook: 3–4 hours or 7–8 hours

You'll Need: slow cooker, heavy-duty aluminum foil, nonstick spray, large bowl

⅕ of recipe:
200 calories
4g total fat
(1.5g sat. fat)
495mg sodium
17g carbs
1g fiber
8.5g sugars
23g protein

1. Fully line a slow cooker with heavy-duty aluminum foil, draping excess foil over the sides. (You'll use the draped foil to lift out the cooked meatloaf.) Spray with nonstick spray.

2. In a large bowl, combine beef, mushrooms, onion, egg whites/substitute, bread crumbs, ¼ cup ketchup, and seasonings. Thoroughly mix.

3. Form into a loaf shape, and place on the foil. Top meatloaf with remaining ¼ cup ketchup.

4. Cover and cook on high for 3–4 hours or on low for 7–8 hours, until cooked through.

MAKES 5 SERVINGS

HG Tip
Looking for a great accompaniment to this meatloaf? Flip to pages 66 and 67 for two tasty takes on mashed potatoes!

classic pot roast

Pictured on page 141

One 3-pound raw boneless chuck beef roast, trimmed of excess fat
1 teaspoon salt, divided
1 teaspoon black pepper, divided
4 cups carrots cut into coins
3 cups roughly chopped onion
2 cups sliced mushrooms
2 cups fat-free beef broth
1 cup celery cut into ½-inch pieces
2 tablespoons tomato paste
1 tablespoon Worcestershire sauce
2 sprigs fresh thyme
1 teaspoon chopped garlic
2 tablespoons cornstarch

1. Spray a slow cooker with nonstick spray.

2. Bring a large skillet sprayed with nonstick spray to high heat. Season roast with ¼ teaspoon salt and ¼ teaspoon pepper. Cook and rotate until all sides are browned, about 5 minutes. Place in the slow cooker.

3. Add all remaining ingredients except cornstarch, including the remaining ¾ teaspoon salt and ¾ teaspoon black pepper. Gently stir.

4. Cook on high for 3–4 hours or on low for 7–8 hours, until roast is cooked through.

5. Turn off slow cooker. In a small bowl, combine cornstarch with 2 tablespoons water. Stir to dissolve. Stir mixture into the liquid in the slow cooker.

6. Let sit, uncovered, until slightly thickened, about 5 minutes.

7. Remove and discard thyme sprigs. Slice meat, and serve topped with veggies and sauce.

MAKES 12 SERVINGS

206 calories

Prep: 15 minutes

Cook: 5 minutes, plus 3–4 hours or 7–8 hours

Cool: 5 minutes

You'll Need: slow cooker, nonstick spray, large skillet, small bowl

¹⁄₁₂ of recipe (about 2½ ounces cooked meat plus broth and veggies):
206 calories
7g total fat
(3g sat. fat)
447mg sodium
11g carbs
2g fiber
4.5g sugars
25.5g protein

 desserts

apple cranberry cobbler cake

Pictured on page 152

Filling

8 cups (about 8 medium) peeled and sliced Granny Smith apples
2 tablespoons cornstarch
½ cup sweetened dried cranberries
3 tablespoons brown sugar
2 teaspoons lemon juice
2 teaspoons vanilla extract
1½ teaspoons cinnamon
¼ teaspoon ground nutmeg
¼ teaspoon salt

Topping

2 cups pancake mix
½ cup unsweetened vanilla almond milk
3 tablespoons whipped butter, melted
¼ cup brown sugar, divided
1 teaspoon cinnamon

1. Spray a slow cooker with nonstick spray. Add apples.

2. In a medium bowl, combine cornstarch with ¾ cup water. Whisk to dissolve. Add remaining filling ingredients. Mix well. Pour mixture over apples. Stir to coat.

3. In a large bowl, combine pancake mix, milk, melted butter, and 2 tablespoons brown sugar. Mix until dough forms. (It will be sticky!) Dollop topping over the filling.

4. Top with cinnamon and remaining 2 tablespoons brown sugar. Cover and cook on high for 2–3 hours, until topping is fully cooked and apples have softened.

5. Remove lid, and turn off slow cooker. Let sit until filling has thickened, about 10 minutes.

MAKES 8 SERVINGS

232 calories

V

Prep: 15 minutes

Cook: 2–3 hours

Cool: 10 minutes

You'll Need: slow cooker, nonstick spray, medium bowl, whisk, large bowl

⅛ of recipe:
232 calories
3.5g total fat
(1.5g sat. fat)
332mg sodium
48g carbs
3g fiber
27.5g sugars
3g protein

Apple Cranberry
Cobbler Cake, page 151

Mixed Berry
Cobbler Cake,
opposite page

mixed berry cobbler cake

Pictured on opposite page

Filling

7 cups frozen mixed berries
½ cup pancake mix
¼ cup natural no-calorie sweetener that measures like sugar

Topping

2 cups pancake mix
½ cup unsweetened vanilla almond milk
3 tablespoons whipped butter, melted
¼ cup natural no-calorie sweetener that measures like sugar, divided
1 teaspoon cinnamon

1. Spray a slow cooker with nonstick spray. Add all filling ingredients, and mix until uniform.

2. To make the topping, in a large bowl, combine pancake mix, milk, melted butter, and 2 tablespoons sweetener. Mix until dough forms. (It will be sticky!) Dollop topping over the filling.

3. In a small bowl, mix remaining 2 tablespoons sweetener with cinnamon. Spoon over topping.

4. Cover and cook on high for 2–3 hours, until berries have softened and topping is fully cooked.

5. Turn off slow cooker. Remove lid, and let sit until filling has thickened, about 10 minutes.

MAKES 8 SERVINGS

---

192 calories

Prep: 10 minutes

Cook: 2–3 hours

Cool: 10 minutes

You'll Need: slow cooker, nonstick spray, large bowl, small bowl

⅛ of recipe
(about ⅔ cup):
192 calories
4g total fat
(1.5g sat. fat)
312mg sodium
48g carbs
5.5g fiber
12.5g sugars
4.5g protein

HG Tip
Enjoy your cobbler cake à la mode!

tropical dump cake

Pictured on pages 156–157

3 cups frozen pineapple chunks

2 cups frozen mango chunks

1½ tablespoons cornstarch

3 packets natural no-calorie sweetener

1¾ cups (about ½ box) natural yellow cake mix

½ cup unsweetened applesauce

2 teaspoons coconut extract

Optional toppings: toasted shredded coconut, light whipped topping

1. Spray a slow cooker with nonstick spray. Add pineapple, mango, cornstarch, and sweetener. Mix well.

2. In a large bowl, combine cake mix, applesauce, and coconut extract. Stir until smooth and uniform.

3. Spread cake batter over the fruit. Cover and cook on high for 2–3 hours or on low for 5–6 hours, until fruit has softened and cake is golden brown and fully cooked.

MAKES 8 SERVINGS

214 calories

Prep: 10 minutes

Cook: 2–3 hours or 5–6 hours

You'll Need: slow cooker, nonstick spray, large bowl

⅛ of recipe (about ¾ cup):
214 calories
1.5g total fat
(0.5g sat. fat)
253mg sodium
48g carbs
2g fiber
31g sugars
1g protein

black forest dump cake

Pictured on pages 156–157

3 cups frozen pitted dark sweet cherries
¼ cup natural no-calorie sweetener that measures like sugar
1 tablespoon cornstarch
1¾ cups (about ½ box) natural devil's food cake mix
½ cup canned pure pumpkin
Optional topping: light whipped topping

1. Spray a slow cooker with nonstick spray. Add cherries, sweetener, and cornstarch. Mix well.

2. In a large bowl, combine cake mix with pumpkin. Stir until mostly smooth and uniform. (Batter will be thick.)

3. Spread cake batter over the cherries. Cover and cook on high for 2–3 hours or on low for 5–6 hours, or until cherry mixture has thickened and cake is fully cooked.

MAKES 8 SERVINGS

180 calories

Prep: 10 minutes

Cook: 2–3 hours or 5–6 hours

You'll Need: slow cooker, nonstick spray, large bowl

⅛ of recipe (about ⅔ cup):
180 calories
2.5g total fat
(1g sat. fat)
290mg sodium
45g carbs
3g fiber
22.5g sugars
2g protein

Tropical Dump Cake,
page 154

Apple & Spice Dump Cake,
page 160

Black Forest Dump Cake, page 155

Strawberry Shortcake Dump Cake, page 159

Chocolate-Covered Strawberry Dump Cake, page 158

chocolate-covered strawberry dump cake

Pictured on pages 156–157

3 cups frozen strawberries
¼ cup natural no-calorie sweetener that measures like sugar
1 tablespoon cornstarch
1¾ cups (about ½ box) natural devil's food cake mix
½ cup canned pure pumpkin
Optional topping: light whipped topping, powdered sugar

1. Spray a slow cooker with nonstick spray. Add strawberries, sweetener, and cornstarch. Mix well.

2. In a large bowl, combine cake mix with pumpkin. Stir until mostly smooth and uniform. (Batter will be thick.)

3. Spread cake batter over the strawberries. Cover and cook on high for 2–3 hours or on low for 5–6 hours, until strawberry mixture has thickened and cake is fully cooked.

MAKES 8 SERVINGS

160 calories

Prep: 10 minutes

Cook: 2–3 hours or 5–6 hours

You'll Need: slow cooker, nonstick spray, large bowl

⅛ of recipe (about ⅔ cup):
160 calories
2g total fat
(1g sat. fat)
290mg sodium
41g carbs
2.5g fiber
18.5g sugars
2g protein

strawberry shortcake dump cake

Pictured on pages 156–157

5 cups frozen strawberries
1 tablespoon cornstarch
3 packets natural no-calorie sweetener
1¾ cups (about ½ box) natural yellow cake mix
½ cup unsweetened applesauce
1 cup light whipped topping (thawed from frozen)

1. Spray a slow cooker with nonstick spray. Add strawberries, cornstarch, and sweetener. Mix well.

2. In a large bowl, combine cake mix with applesauce. Stir until smooth and uniform.

3. Spread cake batter over the strawberries. Cover and cook on high for 2–3 hours or on low for 5–6 hours, until strawberry mixture has thickened and cake is golden brown and fully cooked.

4. Serve topped with whipped topping, 2 tablespoons per serving.

MAKES 8 SERVINGS

199 calories

Prep: 5 minutes

Cook: 2–3 hours or 5–6 hours

You'll Need: slow cooker, nonstick spray, large bowl

⅛ of recipe (about ¾ cup):
199 calories
3g total fat
(1.5g sat. fat)
253mg sodium
42g carbs
2g fiber
22.5g sugars
1g protein

apple & spice dump cake

Pictured on pages 156–157

6 cups (about 6 medium) peeled and sliced Granny Smith apples
2 tablespoons cornstarch
¼ cup natural no-calorie sweetener that measures like sugar
2 teaspoons vanilla extract
1½ teaspoons cinnamon
¼ teaspoon salt
⅛ teaspoon ground nutmeg
1¾ cups (about ½ box) spice cake mix
⅓ cup unsweetened applesauce
Optional topping: light whipped topping

1. Spray a slow cooker with nonstick spray. Add apples.

2. In a medium bowl, combine cornstarch with ½ cup water. Whisk to dissolve. Add sweetener, vanilla extract, cinnamon, salt, and nutmeg. Mix well.

3. Pour cornstarch mixture over apples, and stir to coat.

4. In a large bowl, combine cake mix with applesauce. Stir until smooth and uniform.

5. Spread cake batter over the apples. Cover and cook on high for 2–3 hours or on low for 5–6 hours, until apples have softened and cake is golden brown and fully cooked.

MAKES 8 SERVINGS

172 calories

Prep: 10 minutes

Cook: 2–3 hours or 5–6 hours

You'll Need: slow cooker, nonstick spray, medium bowl, whisk, large bowl

⅛ of recipe (about ¾ cup):
172 calories
2g total fat
(1g sat. fat)
284mg sodium
44.5g carbs
1.5g fiber
22g sugars
1g protein

cake chat

Gone are the days of limited cake mix choices. Look for natural options, organic ones, and even low-sugar mixes that'll seriously slash the sugar counts of these recipes.

What's in a box? About 3–4 cups of cake mix, that's what! Most of these recipes call for 1¾ cups, about half a box worth. While we're talking boxes, ignore any add-ins mentioned on the side. For these recipes, stick to the ingredient list.

scoopable apple pie

Pictured on pages 162–163

8 cups (about 8 medium) peeled and sliced Granny Smith apples
2 tablespoons cornstarch
⅓ cup natural no-calorie sweetener that measures like sugar
2 teaspoons lemon juice
1½ teaspoons cinnamon
1 teaspoon vanilla extract
¼ teaspoon ground nutmeg
¼ teaspoon salt

1. Spray a slow cooker with nonstick spray. Add apples.

2. In a medium bowl, combine cornstarch with ¾ cup water. Whisk to dissolve. Add remaining ingredients. Mix well.

3. Pour cornstarch mixture over apples, and stir to coat.

4. Cover and cook on high for 1½ hours or on low for 3 hours, or until apples have softened and liquid has mostly thickened.

5. Turn off slow cooker. Remove lid, and let sit until thickened, about 10 minutes.

MAKES 8 SERVINGS

64 calories

Prep: 10 minutes

Cook: 1½ hours or 3 hours

Cool: 10 minutes

You'll Need: slow cooker, nonstick spray, medium bowl, whisk

**⅛ of recipe
(about ¾ cup):**
64 calories
<0.5g total fat
(0g sat. fat)
73mg sodium
24g carbs
1.5g fiber
11g sugars
<0.5g protein

Scoopable Peach Pie,
page 164

Scoopable Cherry Pie,
page 165

Scoopable Apple Pie,
page 161

scoopable peach pie

Pictured on pages 162–163

6 cups frozen sliced peaches
2 tablespoons cornstarch
¼ cup natural no-calorie sweetener that measures like sugar
1 teaspoon cinnamon
1 teaspoon vanilla extract
⅛ teaspoon salt

1. Spray a slow cooker with nonstick spray. Add peaches and cornstarch, and stir to coat.

2. Add remaining ingredients. Mix thoroughly.

3. Cover and cook on low for 1½ hours, until peaches have softened and mixture has thickened.

MAKES 6 SERVINGS

75 calories

Prep: 10 minutes

Cook: 1½ hours

You'll Need: slow cooker, nonstick spray

⅙ of recipe
(about ½ cup):
75 calories
0g total fat
(0g sat. fat)
49mg sodium
26.5g carbs
2.5g fiber
12g sugars
1g protein

think outside the pie

These scoopable pies can be enjoyed in an endless number of ways: hot, warm, or chilled! Here's a short list of favorites . . .

over ice cream • topped with crushed graham crackers • over yogurt • topped with whipped topping • over oatmeal • in parfaits • in phyllo shells • topped with crushed cereal • granola

scoopable cherry pie

Pictured on pages 162–163

4 cups frozen pitted dark sweet cherries
2 tablespoons cornstarch
¼ cup natural no-calorie sweetener that measures like sugar
1 teaspoon vanilla extract
½ teaspoon cinnamon
⅛ teaspoon salt

1. Spray a slow cooker with nonstick spray. Add cherries.

2. In a medium bowl, combine cornstarch with ¼ cup water. Whisk to dissolve. Add remaining ingredients. Mix well.

3. Pour cornstarch mixture over cherries, and stir to coat.

4. Add remaining ingredients. Mix thoroughly.

5. Cover and cook on low for 1½ hours, until cherries have softened and mixture has thickened.

MAKES 4 SERVINGS

117 calories

Prep: 10 minutes

Cook: 1½ hours

You'll Need: slow cooker, nonstick spray, medium bowl, whisk

**¼ of recipe
(about ½ cup):**
117 calories
<0.5g total fat
(0g sat. fat)
73mg sodium
38.5g carbs
3g fiber
19g sugars
1g protein

caramelized bananas

5 medium firm bananas
2 ounces (¼ cup) light rum
1 tablespoon cornstarch
⅓ cup brown sugar
3 tablespoons whipped butter, melted
1 teaspoon vanilla extract
½ teaspoon cinnamon
1 ounce (about ¼ cup) chopped walnuts
Serving suggestion: light ice cream

1. Spray a slow cooker with nonstick spray. Slice bananas in half lengthwise, then widthwise. Add sliced bananas to the slow cooker.

2. In a medium bowl, combine rum with cornstarch. Whisk to dissolve. Add sugar, melted butter, vanilla extract, and cinnamon. Mix thoroughly.

3. Pour mixture over the bananas. Cover and cook on low for 2 hours, until bananas have softened and mixture has thickened.

4. Top with walnuts.

MAKES 5 SERVINGS

250 calories

Prep: 10 minutes

Cook: 2 hours

You'll Need: slow cooker, nonstick spray, medium bowl, whisk

⅕ of recipe (½ cup):
250 calories
8g total fat
(2.5g sat. fat)
35mg sodium
38.5g carbs
3.5g fiber
24g sugars
2g protein

pineapple upside-down cake

½ cup brown sugar
¼ cup whipped butter, melted
8 canned pineapple rings packed in juice (not drained)
1¾ cups (about ½ box) natural yellow cake mix
8 maraschino cherries, drained and stems removed
Optional topping: light whipped topping

1. Fully line a slow cooker with heavy-duty aluminum foil, draping excess foil over the sides. (You'll use the draped foil to lift out the cake.) Spray with nonstick spray.

2. In a medium bowl, combine sugar with melted butter. Whisk thoroughly. Transfer to the slow cooker.

3. Add ½ cup juice from the pineapple to a large bowl. Add cake mix. Stir until smooth and uniform.

4. Place pineapple rings in the slow cooker in an even layer. Place a cherry in the center of each ring.

5. Spread cake batter over the fruit. Cover and cook on high for 2–3 hours or on low for 5–6 hours, until cake is golden brown and fully cooked.

6. Immediately run a knife along the edge of the foil to help separate the cake from the foil. Gently lift foil out of the slow cooker.

7. Firmly place a large plate over the foil, and carefully flip so that the plate is on the bottom. Gently lift foil to release cake.

MAKES 8 SERVINGS

237 calories

Prep: 10 minutes

Cook: 2–3 hours or 5–6 hours

You'll Need: slow cooker, heavy-duty aluminum foil, nonstick spray, medium bowl, whisk, large bowl

⅛ of recipe (about ⅔ cup):
237 calories
5g total fat
(2.5g sat. fat)
281mg sodium
47g carbs
1g fiber
32.5g sugars
1g protein

HG Tip
One 20-ounce can of pineapple rings usually has about 10 pineapple rings and 1 cup juice.

All-American Breakfast Dumplings,
page 203

air-fryer recipes

Whether you're an air-fryer expert or haven't even taken yours out of the box, I promise these recipes will soon become favorites! **Air fryers are magical appliances, turning ordinary foods into crispy delights . . . without the excess oil (or deep-frying)** associated with traditional fried food. Before you get started, here's an air-fryer primer.

air-fryer 101

Use a 6-quart or larger air fryer. Air fryers come as tiny as 1-quart capacity. These smaller sizes are excellent for reheating leftovers or cooking for one. But when it comes to these recipes, bigger is better. If your air fryer is small, just work in batches.

Give your food some breathing room. One of the most important aspects of air frying is to leave room for the air to circulate. If you're cooking egg rolls, for example, make sure they're spaced out and not touching. That'll give you the crispiest results without the worry of uneven cooking. If needed, save any remaining food for a second batch.

Your air fryer's BFF: nonstick spray. Always spray the basket with nonstick spray to prevent sticking. In some of these recipes, I also recommend spritzing the food itself to optimize crispiness or browning. Also, consider a non-aerosol spray—these have been known to prolong the life of your air fryer. You can buy refillable misters on Amazon, and you'll find some non-aerosol sprays at the supermarket. Another option: air-fryer liners! They contain holes to help the air circulate, and they make cleanup a breeze.

Shake things up. For perfectly even cooking and crispiness, give the basket a shake (or flip the contents) midway through cooking. Silicone kitchen tongs are perfect for flipping.

Mind the temp. The temperatures shown on the dial vary among devices. If you don't see the suggested cooking temperature on your air fryer, just round to the nearest degree. These recipes were tested with five different air fryers—each one has its own personality, so don't be afraid to check on your food before the suggested cook time. Unlike slow cookers, opening it early won't impact the results.

By the way . . . You can make these recipes even if you don't own an air fryer! Keep reading to learn how to convert these recipes for oven-baked perfection, along with tips for reheating your leftovers!

Chicken Pot Pie Egg Rolls, page 235

oven conversion guide

To make these recipes in an oven, increase the temperature by around 25°F, and raise the cook time by about 25 percent. For example, if you're baking bagels that cook in an air fryer at 360°F for 12–14 minutes, bake them in an oven at 385°F for 15–17 minutes. Keep in mind, this formula is an estimate, as all ovens and air fryers vary. Check on your food to avoid undercooking and overcooking, and ALWAYS ensure that meats, poultry, and fish are fully cooked before consuming.

Don't forget to flip. Air fryers allow air to circulate all around your food, so flipping the food isn't always necessary. Ovens don't offer that particular skill, so flip your food about halfway through baking.

Bonus tools for crispy results. Perforated pans (a.k.a. perforated crisper trays) DO allow air to circulate when you bake food in the oven, mimicking the air-fryer feature. You can find these on Amazon. Another option? Stack a cooling rack over a baking sheet for similar results.

Crunchy Onion Rings, page 205

reheat like a pro

You can reheat your air-fried food right in the air fryer. Start at 380°F for 5 minutes, and adjust as needed. Your toaster oven is another great choice for crispy leftovers!

Sweet Potato & Butternut Fries, page 214

bagels & bagel bites

easy everything bagels

Pictured on pages 176–177

½ cup self-rising flour
½ cup fat-free plain Greek yogurt
1 teaspoon everything bagel seasoning

1. In a large bowl, mix flour and yogurt until dough forms.

2. Shape dough into two bagels. Top with everything bagel seasoning, and press to adhere.

3. Spray an air fryer with nonstick spray. Place bagels in the air fryer, and spray with nonstick spray.

4. Set air fryer to 360°F. Cook until golden brown and cooked through, 12–14 minutes.

MAKES 2 SERVINGS

145 calories

Prep: 10 minutes

Cook: 15 minutes

You'll Need: large bowl, air fryer, nonstick spray

½ of recipe (1 bagel):
145 calories
0g total fat
(0g sat. fat)
541mg sodium
24.5g carbs
<0.5g fiber
2g sugars
8.5g protein

Easy Everything Bagels,
page 175

Cinnamon Raisin
Bagels, page 178

Jalapeño Cheddar
Bagels, page 179

cinnamon raisin bagels

Pictured on pages 176–177

1 tablespoon raisins, chopped
½ cup self-rising flour
½ teaspoon cinnamon
1 packet natural no-calorie sweetener
1 dash salt
½ cup fat-free plain Greek yogurt

1. In a small bowl, soak raisins in hot water until softened, about 5 minutes. Drain excess liquid.

2. In a large bowl, combine flour, cinnamon, sweetener, and salt. Mix well. Add yogurt. Mix until dough forms. Fold in raisins.

3. Shape dough into two bagels.

4. Spray an air fryer with nonstick spray. Place bagels in the air fryer, and spray with nonstick spray.

5. Set air fryer to 360°F. Cook until golden brown and cooked through, 12–14 minutes.

MAKES 2 SERVINGS

158 calories

Prep: 15 minutes

Cook: 15 minutes

You'll Need: small bowl, large bowl, air fryer, nonstick spray

½ of recipe (1 bagel):
158 calories
0g total fat
(0g sat. fat)
460mg sodium
30g carbs
1.5g fiber
5.5g sugars
8.5g protein

jalapeño cheddar bagels

Pictured on pages 176–177

½ cup self-rising flour
¼ teaspoon garlic powder
1 dash salt
½ cup fat-free plain Greek yogurt
1 tablespoon canned diced jalapeño peppers, drained
2 tablespoons shredded reduced-fat cheddar cheese

1. In a large bowl, combine flour, garlic powder, and salt. Mix well. Add yogurt. Mix until dough forms. Fold in jalapeño peppers.

2. Shape dough into two bagels. Top with cheese, and lightly press to adhere.

3. Spray an air fryer with nonstick spray. Place bagels in the air fryer, and spray with nonstick spray.

4. Set air fryer to 360°F. Cook until golden brown and cooked through, 12 14 minutes.

MAKES 2 SERVINGS

160 calories

Prep: 10 minutes

Cook: 15 minutes

You'll Need: large bowl, air fryer, nonstick spray

**½ of recipe
(1 bagel):**
160 calories
1.5g total fat
(1g sat. fat)
565mg sodium
25g carbs
0.5g fiber
2.5g sugars
10g protein

chocolate chip bagel bites

Pictured on pages 182–183

½ **cup self-rising flour**
1 **packet natural no-calorie sweetener**
1 **dash cinnamon**
1 **dash salt**
½ **cup fat-free plain Greek yogurt**
½ **teaspoon vanilla extract**
1 **tablespoon mini semi-sweet chocolate chips**

1. In a large bowl, combine flour, sweetener, cinnamon, and salt. Mix well. Add yogurt and vanilla extract. Mix until dough forms. Fold in chocolate chips.

2. Shape dough into 8 balls, about 2 tablespoons each.

3. Spray an air fryer with nonstick spray. Place bagel bites in the air fryer, and spray with nonstick spray.

4. Set air fryer to 360°F. Cook until golden brown and cooked through, 8–10 minutes.

MAKES 2 SERVINGS

176 calories

Prep: 10 minutes

Cook: 10 minutes

You'll Need: large bowl, air fryer, nonstick spray

½ of recipe (4 bagel bites):
176 calories
2g total fat
(1.5g sat. fat)
458mg sodium
29.5g carbs
0.5g fiber
6.5g sugars
8.5g protein

blueberry bagel bites

Pictured on pages 182–183

½ **cup self-rising flour**
½ **teaspoon cinnamon**
⅛ **teaspoon salt**
½ **cup fat-free blueberry Greek yogurt**
¼ **cup freeze-dried blueberries**

1. In a large bowl, combine flour, cinnamon, and salt. Mix well. Add yogurt. Mix until dough forms. Fold in blueberries.

2. Evenly form into 8 balls, about 2 tablespoons each.

3. Spray an air fryer with nonstick spray. Place bagel bites in the air fryer, and spray with nonstick spray.

4. Set air fryer to 360°F. Cook until golden brown and cooked through, 8–10 minutes.

MAKES 2 SERVINGS

160 calories

Prep: 10 minutes

Cook: 10 minutes

You'll Need: large bowl, air fryer, nonstick spray

½ **of recipe**
(4 bagel bites):
160 calories
0g total fat
(0g sat. fat)
536mg sodium
31g carbs
1g fiber
7g sugars
7g protein

Chocolate Chip Bagel Bites, page 180
Blueberry Bagel Bites, page 181
Apple Pie Cheesecake Bagel Bites, page 184
Strawberry Cheesecake Bagel Bites, page 185
Cheesy Stuffed Bagel Bites, page 186

apple pie cheesecake bagel bites

Pictured on pages 182–183

½ cup self-rising flour
1 packet natural no-calorie sweetener
1¼ teaspoons cinnamon
¼ teaspoon ground nutmeg
⅛ teaspoon salt
½ cup fat-free vanilla Greek yogurt
½ teaspoon vanilla extract
¼ cup finely chopped freeze-dried apples
2 tablespoons light/reduced-fat cream cheese

1. In a large bowl, combine flour, sweetener, cinnamon, nutmeg, and salt. Mix well. Add yogurt and vanilla extract. Mix until dough forms. Fold in apples.

2. Shape dough into 8 balls, about 2 tablespoons each. Press an indentation into each dough ball, and fill with cream cheese, ¾ teaspoon each. Seal dough around filling.

3. Spray an air fryer with nonstick spray. Place bagel bites in the air fryer, and spray with nonstick spray.

4. Set air fryer to 360°F. Cook until golden brown and cooked through, 8–10 minutes.

MAKES 2 SERVINGS

204 calories

Prep: 10 minutes

Cook: 10 minutes

You'll Need: large bowl, air fryer, nonstick spray

**½ of recipe
(4 bagel bites):**
204 calories
3g total fat
(2g sat. fat)
597mg sodium
34.5g carbs
1.5g fiber
9g sugars
8.5g protein

strawberry cheesecake bagel bites

Pictured on pages 182–183

½ **cup self-rising flour**
1 **packet natural no-calorie sweetener**
⅛ **teaspoon salt**
½ **cup fat-free strawberry Greek yogurt**
½ **teaspoon vanilla extract**
¼ **cup chopped freeze-dried strawberries**
2 **tablespoons light/reduced-fat cream cheese**

1. In a large bowl, combine flour, sweetener, and salt. Mix well. Add yogurt and vanilla extract. Mix until dough forms. Fold in strawberries.

2. Shape dough into 8 balls, about 2 tablespoons each. Press an indentation into each dough ball, and fill with cream cheese, ¾ teaspoon each. Seal dough around filling.

3. Spray an air fryer with nonstick spray. Place bagel bites in the air fryer, and spray with nonstick spray.

4. Set air fryer to 360°F. Cook until golden brown and cooked through, 8–10 minutes.

MAKES 2 SERVINGS

216 calories

Prep: 10 minutes

Cook: 10 minutes

You'll Need: large bowl, air fryer, nonstick spray

½ of recipe (4 bagel bites):
216 calories
3g total fat
(1.5g sat. fat)
597mg sodium
36g carbs
1g fiber
10.5g sugars
9.5g protein

cheesy stuffed bagel bites

Pictured on pages 182–183

½ cup self-rising flour
¼ teaspoon garlic powder
¼ teaspoon onion powder
⅛ teaspoon Italian seasoning
½ cup fat-free plain Greek yogurt
1 stick light string cheese, sliced into 8 coins
Optional dip: marinara sauce

1. In a large bowl, mix flour with seasonings. Add yogurt. Mix until dough forms.

2. Shape dough into 8 balls, about 2 tablespoons each. Press an indentation into each dough ball, and fill with a piece of cheese. Seal dough around cheese.

3. Spray an air fryer with nonstick spray. Place bagel bites in the air fryer, and spray with nonstick spray.

4. Set air fryer to 360°F. Cook until golden brown and cooked through, 8–10 minutes.

MAKES 2 SERVINGS

168 calories

Prep: 10 minutes

Cook: 10 minutes

You'll Need: large bowl, air fryer, nonstick spray

**½ of recipe
(4 bagel bites):**
168 calories
1.5g total fat
(0.5g sat. fat)
475mg sodium
25.5g carbs
<0.5g fiber
2.5g sugars
12g protein

HG FYI
Sometimes cheese will ooze out of your bagel bites . . . Deliciousness like this can't always be contained!

all about 2-ingredient dough

A slew of the air-fryer recipes in this cookbook feature 2-ingredient dough, a 1:1 mix of self-rising flour and Greek yogurt. Here are some tips & tricks to know when working with this super-simple and versatile dough . . .

Lightly dust your hands and work surface with flour. The dough is a little sticky, so this will help keep it stuck to itself and NOT to you and your kitchen!

Refrigerated dough is even easier to handle. Once the dough is made, pop it in the refrigerator for at least 5 minutes. Once it has settled and chilled, it'll be easier to shape as needed.

Get creative! You can use the basic dough formula to make your own pizzas, flatbreads, sandwich pockets, and more. Or just stick with my specific recipes . . .

S'mores Chomptarts, page 332

more breakfast dishes ✦✦

french toast sticks

Pictured on opposite page

⅓ cup (about 3 large) egg whites or fat-free liquid egg substitute

2 tablespoons unsweetened vanilla almond milk

1 packet natural no-calorie sweetener

¾ teaspoon vanilla extract

½ teaspoon cinnamon

1 dash salt

2 slices whole-grain bread with 60–80 calories per slice

Optional toppings: natural sugar-free pancake syrup, powdered sugar

1. In a medium bowl, combine all ingredients except bread. Whisk with a fork until uniform.

2. Cut bread into 1-inch-wide strips. Coat with egg mixture.

3. Spray an air fryer with nonstick spray. Place French toast sticks in the air fryer.

4. Set air fryer to 360°F. Cook until golden brown and crispy, 7–9 minutes.

MAKES 1 SERVING

202 calories

Prep: 5 minutes

Cook: 10 minutes

You'll Need: medium bowl, air fryer, nonstick spray

Entire recipe:
202 calories
2g total fat
(0g sat. fat)
533mg sodium
30.5g carbs
6g fiber
4g sugars
14.5g protein

French Toast Sticks,
opposite page

Triple Berry Stuffed
French Toast, page 190

triple berry stuffed french toast

Pictured on page 189

French Toast

⅓ cup (about 3 large) egg whites or fat-free liquid egg substitute
1 tablespoon unsweetened vanilla almond milk
1 packet natural no-calorie sweetener
¼ teaspoon cinnamon
¼ teaspoon vanilla extract
1 dash salt
2 slices whole-grain bread with 60–80 calories per slice

Filling

¼ cup light/low-fat ricotta cheese
1 packet natural no-calorie sweetener
¼ teaspoon vanilla extract
1 dash cinnamon
¼ cup mixed berries (fresh or thawed from frozen)
Optional toppings: powdered sugar, natural sugar-free pancake syrup

1. In a wide bowl, combine all French toast ingredients except bread. Whisk with a fork until uniform.

2. Coat bread with egg mixture.

3. Spray an air fryer with nonstick spray. Place French toast in the air fryer.

4. Set air fryer to 360°F. Cook until golden brown and crispy, 10–12 minutes.

5. In a small bowl, combine all filling ingredients except berries. Mix until smooth and uniform. Fold in berries.

6. Spread one slice of French toast with the filling. Top with the other slice, and lightly press to seal.

MAKES 1 SERVING

---

262 calories

Prep: 10 minutes

Cook: 15 minutes

You'll Need: wide bowl, air fryer, nonstick spray, small bowl

Entire recipe:
262 calories
4.5g total fat
(1.5g sat. fat)
605mg sodium
38g carbs
7g fiber
9g sugars
20.5g protein

peanut butter breakfast cookies

Pictured on page 192

¼ cup mashed ripe banana
¼ cup old-fashioned oats
1½ tablespoons powdered peanut butter
1 teaspoon creamy peanut butter
½ packet natural no-calorie sweetener
1 dash salt

1. Line an air fryer with parchment paper, leaving room for air to circulate.

2. In a medium bowl, combine all ingredients. Add 1½ tablespoons water, and mix until uniform.

3. Form three 2-inch cookies, and place them on the parchment paper in the air fryer.

4. Set air fryer to 300°F. Cook until a toothpick inserted in the center of a cookie comes out clean, about 10 minutes.

MAKES 1 SERVING

200 calories

Prep: 10 minutes

Cook: 10 minutes

You'll Need: air fryer, parchment paper, medium bowl, toothpick

Entire recipe:
200 calories
5.5g total fat
(0.5g sat. fat)
221mg sodium
32g carbs
5g fiber
9g sugars
9g protein

Oatmeal Raisin
Breakfast Cookies,
opposite page

Sweet Cinnamon Rolls,
page 194

Peanut Butter Breakfast
Cookies, page 191

oatmeal raisin breakfast cookies

Pictured on opposite page

⅓ cup old-fashioned oats
¼ cup unsweetened applesauce
½ teaspoon cinnamon
¼ teaspoon vanilla extract
1 dash ground nutmeg
1 dash salt
1½ tablespoons raisins

1. Line an air fryer with parchment paper, leaving room for air to circulate.

2. In a medium bowl, combine all ingredients except raisins. Add 1 tablespoon water, and mix until uniform. Fold in raisins.

3. Form three 2-inch cookies, and place them on the parchment paper in the air fryer.

4. Set air fryer to 300°F. Cook until a toothpick inserted in the center of a cookie comes out clean, about 10 minutes.

MAKES 1 SERVING

182 calories

Prep: 10 minutes

Cook: 10 minutes

You'll Need: air fryer, parchment paper, medium bowl, toothpick

Entire recipe:
182 calories
2g total fat
(<0.5g sat. fat)
159mg sodium
37.5g carbs
5g fiber
16g sugars
4g protein

sweet cinnamon rolls

Pictured on page 192

½ cup self-rising flour
½ cup fat-free plain Greek yogurt
2 teaspoons whipped butter (room temperature)
½ teaspoon cinnamon
1 packet natural no-calorie sweetener
3 tablespoons powdered sugar
1½ teaspoons unsweetened vanilla almond milk

1. In a large bowl, mix flour and yogurt until dough forms.

2. Roll out dough into a large rectangle, about 7 inches by 5 inches and ¼-inch thick.

3. Spread butter onto the dough, leaving a ½-inch border. Top with cinnamon and sweetener.

4. Tightly roll up the dough width-wise into a log, and pinch the seam to seal. Turn log seam side down, and cut into 4 rolls.

5. Spray an air fryer with nonstick spray. Place rolls in the air fryer, and spray with nonstick spray.

6. Set air fryer to 360°F. Cook until light golden brown and cooked through, about 10 minutes.

7. In a small bowl, mix sugar with milk until uniform. Drizzle over rolls.

MAKES 4 SERVINGS

104 calories

Prep: 10 minutes

Cook: 10 minutes

You'll Need: large bowl, air fryer, nonstick spray, small bowl

¼ of recipe
(1 roll):
104 calories
1g total fat
(0.5g sat. fat)
200mg sodium
18.5g carbs
0.5g fiber
7g sugars
4g protein

bacon, egg & cheddar breakfast wrap

Pictured on pages 196–197

½ cup (about 4 large) egg whites or fat-free liquid egg substitute
⅛ teaspoon garlic powder
⅛ teaspoon onion powder
2 tablespoons shredded reduced-fat cheddar cheese
1 teaspoon precooked crumbled bacon
1 low-carb flour tortilla with 100 calories or less

1. Spray a microwave-safe mug with nonstick spray. Add egg whites/substitute, garlic powder, and onion powder. Microwave for 1 minute.

2. Mix well. Microwave for 30 seconds, or until cooked through.

3. Stir in cheese and bacon.

4. Place scramble along the center of the tortilla. Wrap tortilla up like a burrito: First fold in the sides, then roll it up from the bottom.

5. Spray an air fryer with nonstick spray. Place wrap in the air fryer, seam side down.

6. Set air fryer to 375°F. Cook until golden brown and crispy, about 5 minutes.

MAKES 1 SERVING

221 calories

 5i **15m**

Prep: 5 minutes

Cook: 10 minutes

You'll Need:
microwave-safe mug, nonstick spray, air fryer

Entire recipe:
221 calories
6.5g total fat
(3.5g sat. fat)
639mg sodium
21.5g carbs
7.5g fiber
1g sugars
22g protein

Spinach, Egg & Feta
Breakfast Wrap,
page 198

Bacon, Egg
& Cheddar
Breakfast
Wrap,
page 195

California Breakfast Burrito,
page 199

spinach, egg & feta breakfast wrap

Pictured on pages 196–197

⅓ cup (about 3 large) egg whites or fat-free liquid egg substitute
⅛ teaspoon garlic powder
⅛ teaspoon onion powder
1 dash salt
1 cup roughly chopped spinach
2 tablespoons crumbled feta cheese
2 tablespoons bagged or drained sun-dried tomatoes, chopped
1 low-carb flour tortilla with 100 calories or less

1. Bring a skillet sprayed with nonstick spray to medium heat. Add egg whites/substitute, garlic powder, onion powder, and salt. Cook and scramble until fully cooked, about 3 minutes.

2. Add spinach. Cook and stir until wilted, about 1 minute.

3. Remove skillet from heat. Fold in feta and tomatoes.

4. Place scramble along the center of the tortilla. Wrap tortilla up like a burrito: First fold in the sides, then roll it up from the bottom.

5. Spray an air fryer with nonstick spray. Place wrap in an air fryer, seam side down.

6. Set air fryer to 375°F. Cook until golden brown and crispy, about 5 minutes.

MAKES 1 SERVING

231 calories

Prep: 5 minutes

Cook: 10 minutes

You'll Need: skillet, nonstick spray, air fryer

Entire recipe:
231 calories
6g total fat
(3.5g sat. fat)
776mg sodium
29.5g carbs
10g fiber
5.5g sugars
17.5g protein

california breakfast burrito

Pictured on pages 196–197

¼ cup chopped mushrooms

¼ cup seeded and chopped tomato

¼ cup (about 2 large) egg whites or fat-free liquid egg substitute

⅛ teaspoon garlic powder

⅛ teaspoon onion powder

2 tablespoons canned black beans, drained and rinsed

2 tablespoons shredded reduced-fat Mexican-blend cheese

1 ounce (about 2 tablespoons) chopped avocado

1 low-carb flour tortilla with 100 calories or less

1. Bring a skillet sprayed with nonstick spray to medium heat. Add mushrooms and tomato. Cook and stir until slightly softened, about 2 minutes. Add egg whites/substitute, garlic powder, and onion powder. Cook and scramble until fully cooked, about 3 minutes.

2. Remove skillet from heat. Fold in black beans and cheese.

3. Place scramble along the center of the tortilla. Top with avocado. Wrap tortilla up by first folding the sides, then rolling it up from the bottom.

4. Spray an air fryer with nonstick spray. Place wrap in the air fryer, seam side down.

5. Set air fryer to 375°F. Cook until golden brown and crispy, about 5 minutes.

MAKES 1 SERVING

264 calories

Prep: 10 minutes

Cook: 10 minutes

You'll Need: skillet, nonstick spray, air fryer

Entire recipe:
264 calories
11g total fat
(3.5g sat. fat)
554mg sodium
30.5g carbs
11.5g fiber
2.5g sugars
17.5g protein

homestyle breakfast foil pack

Pictured on opposite page

5 ounces (about ½ medium) russet potato, cubed
½ cup roughly chopped bell pepper
¼ cup roughly chopped onion
1 teaspoon olive oil
¼ teaspoon garlic powder
¼ teaspoon paprika
⅛ teaspoon salt
⅛ teaspoon black pepper
1 large egg
Optional topping: chopped chives

1. Cut a piece of heavy-duty aluminum foil into a square about the size of your air fryer basket. Fold up the sides, and spray with nonstick spray.

2. Place potato, bell pepper, and onion in the foil pack. Drizzle with oil, and top with seasonings. Gently toss to coat.

3. Transfer foil pack to an air fryer.

4. Set air fryer to 390°F. Cook until potato is golden brown and crispy, about 9 minutes.

5. Break egg over the contents of the foil. Cook until egg white is cooked through and yolk is cooked to your preference, about 4 minutes.

MAKES 1 SERVING

264 calories

Prep: 10 minutes

Cook: 15 minutes

You'll Need: heavy-duty aluminum foil, nonstick spray, air fryer

Entire recipe:
264 calories
9.5g total fat
(2g sat. fat)
374mg sodium
34.5g carbs
4g fiber
5.5g sugars
10.5g protein

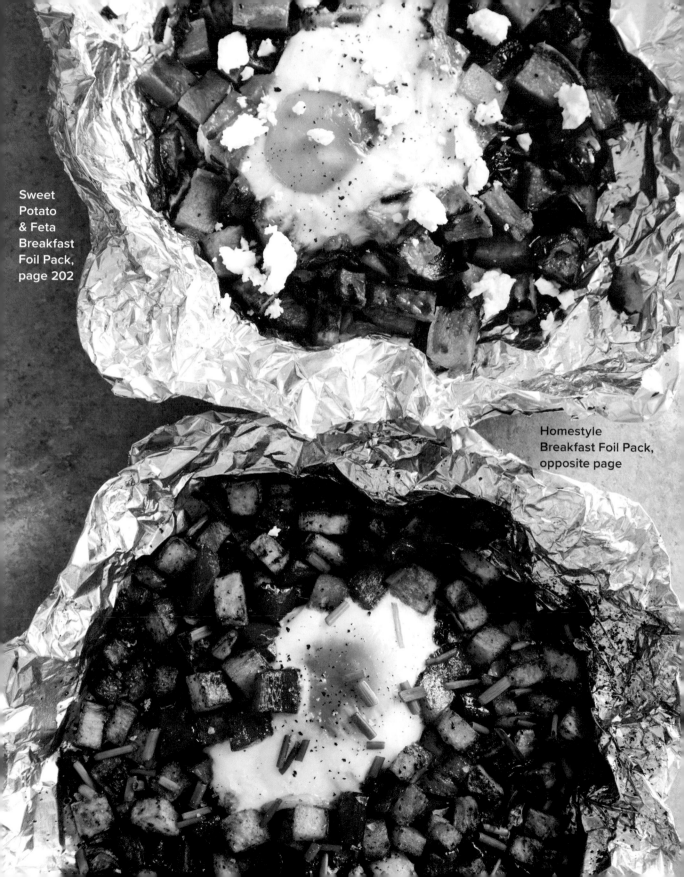

Sweet Potato & Feta Breakfast Foil Pack, page 202

Homestyle Breakfast Foil Pack, opposite page

sweet potato & feta breakfast foil pack

Pictured on page 201

5 ounces (about ½ medium) sweet potato, cubed
½ cup roughly chopped red onion
1 teaspoon olive oil
¼ teaspoon garlic powder
¼ teaspoon onion powder
⅛ teaspoon salt
⅛ teaspoon black pepper
1 large egg
2 tablespoons crumbled feta cheese

1. Cut heavy-duty aluminum foil into a square about the size of your air fryer basket. Fold up the sides, and spray with nonstick spray.

2. Place potato and onion in the foil pack. Drizzle with oil, and top with seasonings. Gently toss to coat.

3. Transfer foil pack to an air fryer.

4. Set air fryer to 390°F. Cook until potato is golden brown and crispy, about 9 minutes.

5. Break egg over the contents of the foil pack. Cook until egg white is cooked through and yolk is cooked to your preference, about 4 minutes.

6. Top with feta.

MAKES 1 SERVING

310 calories

5i **30m** **V** **GF**

Prep: 10 minutes

Cook: 15 minutes

You'll Need: heavy-duty aluminum foil, nonstick spray, air fryer

Entire recipe:
310 calories
12g total fat
(4g sat. fat)
612mg sodium
38.5g carbs
5.5g fiber
10g sugars
11.5g protein

all-american breakfast dumplings

Pictured on page 170

½ cup (about 4 large) egg whites or fat-free liquid egg substitute
1 tablespoon light/reduced-fat cream cheese
1 dash salt
1 tablespoon precooked crumbled bacon
8 gyoza or wonton wrappers

1. Spray a microwave-safe mug with nonstick spray. Add egg whites/substitute, cream cheese, and salt. Microwave for 1 minute.

2. Mix well. Microwave for 30 seconds, or until cooked through.

3. Stir in bacon. Let cool slightly, about 5 minutes.

4. Top one wrapper with ⅛ of the egg scramble, about 1 tablespoon. Moisten the edges with water, and fold wrapper in half, enclosing the filling. Press firmly on the edges to seal. Repeat to make seven more dumplings.

5. Spray an air fryer with nonstick spray. Place dumplings in the air fryer, and spray with nonstick spray.

6. Set air fryer to 370°F. Cook until golden brown and crispy, about 4 minutes.

MAKES 1 SERVING

253 calories

Prep: 10 minutes

Cook: 10 minutes

Cool: 5 minutes

You'll Need:
microwave-safe mug, nonstick spray, air fryer

Entire recipe:
253 calories
4.5g total fat
(2.5g sat. fat)
763mg sodium
30g carbs
1g fiber
1.5g sugars
20.5g protein

apps & sides

easy mozzarella sticks

Pictured on pages 206–207

4 sticks light string cheese
1 tablespoon whole wheat flour
¼ cup panko bread crumbs
¼ teaspoon garlic powder
¼ teaspoon Italian seasoning
¼ teaspoon onion powder
⅛ teaspoon salt
⅛ teaspoon black pepper
2 tablespoons (about 1 large) egg white or fat-free liquid egg substitute

1. Cut string cheese sticks in half widthwise. Place them in a large sealable bag or container. Add flour. Seal bag/container, and shake to coat.

2. In a wide bowl, mix bread crumbs with seasonings. Place egg white/substitute in a second wide bowl. Coat cheese sticks with the egg, followed by the seasoned bread crumbs.

3. Spray an air fryer with nonstick spray. Place cheese sticks in the air fryer, and spray with nonstick spray.

4. Set air fryer to 390°F. Cook until golden brown and crispy, 5–7 minutes.

MAKES 2 SERVINGS

169 calories

5i 30m V

Prep: 10 minutes

Cook: 10 minutes

You'll Need: large sealable bag or container, 2 wide bowls, air fryer, nonstick spray

½ of recipe (4 pieces):
169 calories
5.5g total fat
(3g sat. fat)
570mg sodium
11g carbs
0.5g fiber
0.5g sugars
17g protein

crunchy onion rings

Pictured on pages 206–207

1 large (about 14-ounce) onion
2 tablespoons whole wheat flour
⅔ cup panko bread crumbs
1 teaspoon garlic powder
1 teaspoon onion powder
¼ teaspoon salt
⅛ teaspoon black pepper
¼ cup (about 2 large) egg whites or fat-free liquid egg substitute

1. Slice off onion ends, and remove outer layer. Cut into ½-inch-wide slices, and separate into rings.

2. Place onion rings in a large sealable bag or container. Add flour. Seal bag/container, and shake to coat.

3. In a wide bowl, mix bread crumbs with seasonings. Place egg white/substitute in a second wide bowl. Coat onion rings with the egg, followed by the seasoned bread crumbs.

4. Spray an air fryer with nonstick spray. Place half of the onion rings in the air fryer, and spray with nonstick spray.

5. Set air fryer to 390°F. Cook until golden brown and crispy, 12–15 minutes, flipping halfway through.

6. Repeat with remaining onion rings.

MAKES 2 SERVINGS

159 calories

Prep: 15 minutes

Cook: 30 minutes

You'll Need: large sealable bag or container, 2 wide bowls, air fryer, nonstick spray

½ of recipe (about 12 rings):
159 calories
0.5g total fat
(0g sat. fat)
405mg sodium
30.5g carbs
2.5g fiber
5g sugars
7.5g protein

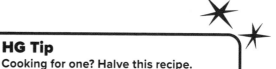

HG Tip
Cooking for one? Halve this recipe.
(Bonus: Half the cook time!)

Easy Mozzarella Sticks, page 204

Crispy Jalapeño Poppers, page 209

Popcorn Shrimp, page 210

Crunchy Onion
Rings, page 205

Faux-Fried Pickle Chips,
page 208

faux-fried pickle chips

Pictured on pages 206–207

⅓ cup panko bread crumbs
¼ teaspoon garlic powder
¼ teaspoon onion powder
1 dash cayenne pepper
1 dash salt
1 dash black pepper
¼ cup (about 2 large) egg whites or fat-free liquid egg substitute
24 hamburger dill pickle chips, blotted dry

1. In a wide bowl, mix bread crumbs and seasonings. Place egg whites/substitute in a second wide bowl. Coat pickle chips with the egg, followed by the seasoned bread crumbs.

2. Spray an air fryer with nonstick spray. Place pickle chips in the air fryer, and spray with nonstick spray.

3. Set air fryer to 390°F. Cook until golden brown and crispy, 3–4 minutes.

MAKES 2 SERVINGS

59 calories

Prep: 10 minutes

Cook: 5 minutes

You'll Need: 2 wide bowls, air fryer, nonstick spray

½ of recipe (12 pickle chips):
59 calories
<0.5g total fat
(0g sat. fat)
658mg sodium
10.5g carbs
1g fiber
1.5g sugars
3g protein

crispy jalapeño poppers

Pictured on pages 206–207

¼ cup whipped cream cheese
2 tablespoons shredded reduced-fat cheddar cheese
¼ teaspoon garlic powder, divided
¼ teaspoon onion powder, divided
⅓ cup panko bread crumbs
⅛ teaspoon salt
⅛ teaspoon black pepper
¼ cup (about 2 large) egg whites or fat-free liquid egg substitute
3 jalapeño peppers

1. In a small bowl, combine cream cheese, cheddar, ⅛ teaspoon garlic powder, and ⅛ teaspoon onion powder. Mix thoroughly.

2. In a wide bowl, combine bread crumbs, salt, black pepper, remaining ⅛ teaspoon garlic powder, and remaining ⅛ teaspoon onion powder. Mix well.

3. Place egg whites/substitute in a second wide bowl.

4. Halve jalapeño peppers lengthwise, and remove seeds and stems. Spread cheese mixture into the pepper halves.

5. Coat pepper halves with the egg, followed by the seasoned bread crumbs.

6. Spray an air fryer with nonstick spray. Place pepper halves in the air fryer, and spray with nonstick spray.

7. Set air fryer to 390°F. Cook until golden brown, about 6 minutes.

MAKES 2 SERVINGS

134 calories

5i 30m V

Prep: 15 minutes

Cook: 10 minutes

You'll Need: small bowl, 2 wide bowls, air fryer, nonstick spray

½ of recipe (3 poppers):
134 calories
6g total fat
(3.5g sat. fat)
369mg sodium
12g carbs
1g fiber
2.5g sugars
7.5g protein

HG Tip
Always wear gloves when handling hot peppers, and avoid touching your eyes. After halving the peppers, run them under water to easily remove the seeds and membrane.

popcorn shrimp

Pictured on pages 206–207

6 ounces (about 18) raw medium shrimp, peeled, tails removed, deveined
2 tablespoons whole wheat flour
¼ cup panko bread crumbs
1 teaspoon garlic powder
¼ teaspoon chili powder
¼ teaspoon salt
1 dash black pepper
¼ cup (about 2 large) egg whites or fat-free liquid egg substitute

1. Place shrimp in a large sealable bag or container. Add flour. Seal bag/container, and shake to coat.

2. In a wide bowl, mix bread crumbs and seasonings. Place egg white/substitute in a second wide bowl. Coat shrimp with the egg, followed by the seasoned bread crumbs.

3. Spray an air fryer with nonstick spray. Place shrimp in the air fryer, and spray with nonstick spray.

4. Set air fryer to 390°F. Cook until crispy and cooked through, 8–10 minutes.

MAKES 2 SERVINGS

156 calories

Prep: 10 minutes

Cook: 10 minutes

You'll Need: large sealable bag or container, 2 wide bowls, air fryer, nonstick spray

½ of recipe (about 9 shrimp):
156 calories
1g total fat
(<0.5g sat. fat)
623mg sodium
13.5g carbs
1.5g fiber
1g sugars
21g protein

spicy buffalo cauliflower

Pictured on pages 212–213

¼ cup whole wheat flour
1 teaspoon garlic powder
1 teaspoon onion powder
¼ teaspoon paprika
⅛ teaspoon cayenne pepper
¼ cup (about 2 large) egg whites or fat-free liquid egg substitute
3 cups cauliflower florets
2 tablespoons Frank's RedHot Original Cayenne Pepper Sauce

1. In a large sealable bag or container, combine flour and seasonings. Seal bag/container, and shake to mix.

2. Place egg white/substitute in a wide bowl. Coat cauliflower with egg, and transfer to the bag/container. Seal bag/container, and shake to coat.

3. Spray an air fryer with nonstick spray. Place cauliflower florets in the air fryer, and spray with nonstick spray.

4. Set air fryer to 390°F. Cook until golden brown and crispy, about 15 minutes.

5. In a small bowl, mix hot sauce with 2 teaspoons water.

6. Transfer cauliflower to a large bowl. Add sauce, and gently toss to coat.

MAKES 2 SERVINGS

120 calories

Prep: 10 minutes

Cook: 15 minutes

You'll Need: large sealable bag or container, wide bowl, air fryer, nonstick spray, small bowl, large bowl

½ of recipe (about 1 cup):
120 calories
0.5g total fat
(<0.5g sat. fat)
673mg sodium
21.5g carbs
5.5g fiber
4g sugars
8.5g protein

Sweet Potato & Butternut Fries,
page 214

Spicy Buffalo
Cauliflower,
page 211

Crispy Brussels
Sprouts & Bacon,
page 216

Crispy
Mushrooms,
page 215

sweet potato & butternut fries

Pictured on pages 212–213

**6 ounces (about ¼ medium) butternut squash, cut into
  fry-shaped spears**
**6 ounces (about ½ medium) sweet potato, peeled and cut into
  fry-shaped spears**
⅛ teaspoon salt

1. Thoroughly pat squash and sweet potato dry. Season with salt.

2. Spray an air fryer with nonstick spray. Place fries in the air fryer, and spray with nonstick spray.

3. Set air fryer to 390°F. Cook until golden brown and crispy, 14–16 minutes, flipping halfway through.

MAKES 2 SERVINGS

110 calories

Prep: 10 minutes

Cook: 20 minutes

You'll Need: air fryer, nonstick spray

½ of recipe:
110 calories
<0.5g total fat
(0g sat. fat)
196mg sodium
26.5g carbs
4g fiber
5.5g sugars
2g protein

HG Tips
Look for a long narrow squash—perfect for fry making! Use a crinkle cutter for that authentic French fry shape and added crispiness!

crispy mushrooms

Pictured on pages 212–213

3 tablespoons panko bread crumbs
1 tablespoon grated Parmesan cheese
1 teaspoon Italian seasoning
½ teaspoon garlic powder
½ teaspoon onion powder
¼ teaspoon salt
1 dash black pepper
¼ cup (about 2 large) egg whites or fat-free liquid egg substitute
8 medium baby bella mushrooms

1. In a wide bowl, combine bread crumbs, Parm, and seasonings. Mix well.

2. Place egg whites/substitute in a second wide bowl. Coat mushrooms with the egg, followed by seasoned bread crumbs.

3. Spray an air fryer with nonstick spray. Place mushrooms in the air fryer, and spray with nonstick spray.

4. Set air fryer to 390°F. Cook until golden brown and crispy, 7–8 minutes.

MAKES 2 SERVINGS

71 calories

 5i 30m

Prep: 10 minutes

Cook: 10 minutes

You'll Need: 2 wide bowls, air fryer, nonstick spray

½ of recipe (4 mushrooms):
71 calories
1.5g total fat
(0.5g sat. fat)
412mg sodium
8.5g carbs
0.5g fiber
2g sugars
6g protein

crispy brussels sprouts & bacon

Pictured on pages 212–213

1 tablespoon balsamic vinegar
1½ teaspoons Dijon mustard
1½ teaspoons olive oil
¼ teaspoon garlic powder
⅛ teaspoon black pepper
8 ounces Brussels sprouts, trimmed and halved
2 slices center-cut bacon or turkey bacon, chopped

1. In a large bowl, combine vinegar, mustard, oil, garlic powder, and pepper. Whisk thoroughly. Add Brussels sprouts and bacon, and toss to coat.

2. Spray an air fryer with nonstick spray. Place Brussels sprouts and bacon in the air fryer, and spray with nonstick spray.

3. Set air fryer to 375°F. Cook until golden brown and crispy, about 10 minutes, shaking halfway through.

MAKES 2 SERVINGS

120 calories

Prep: 5 minutes

Cook: 10 minutes

You'll Need: large bowl, whisk, air fryer, nonstick spray

**½ of recipe
(about 2 cups):**
120 calories
6g total fat
(1g sat. fat)
250mg sodium
12g carbs
4.5g fiber
3.5g sugars
6.5g protein

cheesy bacon dumplings

Pictured on pages 218–219

¼ cup whipped cream cheese

2 tablespoons chopped scallions

1 tablespoon precooked crumbled bacon

⅛ teaspoon garlic powder

⅛ teaspoon onion powder

4 gyoza or wonton wrappers

1. In a small bowl, combine all ingredients except wrappers. Mix until uniform.

2. Top one wrapper with ¼ of the cream cheese mixture, about 1 tablespoon. Moisten the edges with water, and fold wrapper in half, enclosing the filling. Press firmly on the edges to seal. Repeat to make three more dumplings.

3. Spray an air fryer with nonstick spray. Place dumplings in the air fryer, and spray with nonstick spray.

4. Set air fryer to 370°F. Cook until golden brown and crispy, about 4 minutes.

MAKES 1 SERVING

200 calories

Prep: 10 minutes

Cook: 5 minutes

You'll Need: small bowl, air fryer, nonstick spray

Entire recipe:
200 calories
9.5g total fat
(6g sat. fat)
456mg sodium
20g carbs
1g fiber
3g sugars
7g protein

BBQ Chicken
Dumplings, page 220

Cheesy Bacon
Dumplings, page 217

Chicken Potstickers,
page 221

Air-Fried
Ravioli,
page 222

Pizza Sticks,
page 223

BBQ chicken dumplings

Pictured on pages 218–219

2 ounces cooked and finely chopped skinless chicken breast
2 tablespoons chopped scallions
1 tablespoon BBQ sauce
1½ teaspoons whipped cream cheese
⅛ teaspoon garlic powder
⅛ teaspoon onion powder
6 gyoza or wonton wrappers

1. Place all ingredients except wrappers in a medium bowl. Mix until uniform.

2. Top one wrapper with ¼ of the chicken mixture, about 1 tablespoon. Moisten the edges with water, and fold wrapper in half, enclosing the filling. Press firmly on the edges to seal. Repeat to make five more dumplings.

3. Spray an air fryer with nonstick spray. Place dumplings in the air fryer, and spray with nonstick spray.

4. Set air fryer to 370°F. Cook until golden brown and crispy, about 4 minutes.

MAKES 2 SERVINGS

126 calories

Prep: 10 minutes

Cook: 5 minutes

You'll Need: medium bowl, air fryer, nonstick spray

½ of recipe (3 dumplings):
126 calories
1.5g total fat
(0.5g sat. fat)
206mg sodium
16g carbs
0.5g fiber
3.5g sugars
10g protein

chicken potstickers

Pictured on pages 218–219

2 ounces raw extra-lean ground chicken (at least 98% lean)

2 tablespoons canned sliced water chestnuts, drained and chopped

1 tablespoon chopped scallions

2 teaspoons sweet chili sauce, or more for dipping

1½ teaspoons dried minced onion

1 teaspoon reduced-sodium soy sauce, or more for dipping

½ teaspoon chopped garlic

¼ teaspoon ground ginger

8 gyoza or wonton wrappers

1. In a medium bowl, combine all ingredients except wrappers. Mix well.

2. Top one wrapper with ⅛ of the mixture, about 1 tablespoon. Moisten the edges with water, and fold in half, enclosing the filling. Press firmly on the edges to seal. Repeat to make seven more potstickers.

3. Spray an air fryer with nonstick spray. Place potstickers in the air fryer, and spray with nonstick spray.

4. Set air fryer to 390°F. Cook until chicken is cooked through and wrappers are golden brown and crispy, about 5 minutes.

MAKES 2 SERVINGS

127 calories

 30m

Prep: 15 minutes

Cook: 5 minutes

You'll Need: medium bowl, air fryer, nonstick spray

½ of recipe (4 potstickers):
127 calories
0.5g total fat
(0g sat. fat)
264mg sodium
20g carbs
1g fiber
4g sugars
9g protein

air-fried ravioli

Pictured on pages 218–219

⅓ cup light/low-fat ricotta cheese

⅓ cup shredded part-skim mozzarella cheese

½ teaspoon chopped garlic

¼ teaspoon onion powder

⅛ teaspoon Italian seasoning

⅛ teaspoon salt

1 dash ground nutmeg

8 gyoza or wonton wrappers

¼ cup marinara sauce with 70 calories or less per ½-cup serving

1. In a medium bowl, combine all ingredients except wrappers and marinara sauce. Mix well.

2. Top a wrapper with ⅛ of the mixture, about 1 tablespoon. Moisten the edges with water, and fold in half, enclosing the filling. Press firmly on the edges to seal. Repeat to make seven more ravioli.

3. Spray an air fryer with nonstick spray. Place ravioli in the air fryer, and spray with nonstick spray.

4. Set air fryer to 370°F. Cook until golden brown and crispy, about 4 minutes.

5. Place marinara sauce in a microwave-safe bowl. Microwave until hot, about 30 seconds. Serve with ravioli for dipping.

MAKES 2 SERVINGS

187 calories

Prep: 15 minutes

Cook: 5 minutes

You'll Need: medium bowl, air fryer, nonstick spray, microwave-safe bowl

½ of recipe (4 ravioli):
187 calories
6g total fat
(3.5g sat. fat)
563mg sodium
21.5g carbs
1.5g fiber
4.5g sugars
11.5g protein

pizza sticks

Pictured on pages 218–219

12 slices (about ¾ ounce) turkey pepperoni
6 egg roll wrappers
6 sticks light string cheese
Optional dip: marinara sauce

1. Lay 2 pepperoni slices side by side on an egg roll wrapper, a little below the center. Top with a stick of string cheese. Moisten wrapper edges with water. Fold the sides in toward the middle, and roll up tightly around the string cheese. Seal with a dab of water. Repeat to make five more sticks.

2. Spray an air fryer with nonstick spray. Place pizza sticks in the air fryer, and spray with nonstick spray.

3. Set air fryer to 360°F. Cook until golden brown and crispy, 6–8 minutes.

MAKES 6 SERVINGS

127 calories

 5i 30m

Prep: 10 minutes

Cook: 10 minutes

You'll Need: air fryer, nonstick spray

⅙ of recipe (1 stick):
127 calories
3.5g total fat
(1.5g sat. fat)
377mg sodium
14g carbs
0.5g fiber
0.5g sugars
10g protein

that's a wrap!

All about gyoza wrappers, wonton wrappers & egg roll wrappers

- **These paper-thin wrappers are typically made from wheat flour and used in Asian-style dishes.** I love to get creative with them and incorporate unexpected flavors!

- **Gyoza wrappers are small and round.** Wonton wrappers are similar in size but square. Egg roll wrappers are square and about twice the size of wonton wrappers.

- **Look for these wrappers in the refrigerated section of the supermarket near the tofu.**

- **Once opened, they'll stay fresh in the fridge for about a week.** Simply seal them in an airtight bag or container.

- **You can freeze them too!** Spread a tiny bit of flour or cornstarch over each sheet, or cover with parchment paper. Then restack, and place in an airtight bag or container. This will make them easy to separate once thawed.

- **Check the index for more recipes made with these wrap stars!**

white pizza stuffed mushrooms

8 medium baby bella mushrooms
¼ cup shredded part-skim mozzarella cheese
2 tablespoons light/low-fat ricotta cheese
1 tablespoon chopped fresh basil
1 tablespoon light/reduced-fat cream cheese
½ teaspoon garlic powder
1 dash salt

1. Remove stems from mushrooms. Finely chop stems.

2. In a small bowl, combine mozzarella, ricotta, basil, cream cheese, garlic powder, and salt. Mix well. Stir in chopped mushroom stems. Evenly distribute among mushroom caps.

3. Spray an air fryer with nonstick spray. Place mushrooms in the air fryer.

4. Set air fryer to 390°F. Cook until mushrooms are tender and filling is hot, about 8 minutes.

MAKES 2 SERVINGS

88 calories

Prep: 5 minutes

Cook: 10 minutes

You'll Need: small bowl, air fryer, nonstick spray

½ of recipes (4 mushrooms):
88 calories
4.5g total fat
(3g sat. fat)
228mg sodium
5g carbs
0.5g fiber
2.5g sugars
7.5g protein

small bites

ranchy chicken nuggets

Pictured on pages 228–229

⅓ **cup panko bread crumbs**
1 tablespoon grated Parmesan cheese
1 tablespoon ranch dressing/dip seasoning mix
¼ **cup (about 2 large) egg whites or fat-free liquid egg substitute**
8 ounces raw boneless skinless chicken breast, cut into 10 nuggets
Optional dips: BBQ sauce, light ranch dressing

1. In a wide bowl, combine bread crumbs, Parm, and seasoning mix. Mix well.

2. Place egg whites/substitute in a second wide bowl. Coat chicken with egg, followed by the seasoned bread crumbs.

3. Spray an air fryer with nonstick spray. Place chicken nuggets in the air fryer, and spray with nonstick spray.

4. Set air fryer to 360°F. Cook until crispy and cooked through, about 12 minutes.

MAKES 2 SERVINGS

---

222 calories

5i **30m**

Prep: 10 minutes

Cook: 15 minutes

You'll Need: 2 wide bowls, air fryer, nonstick spray

½ of recipe (5 nuggets):
222 calories
4.5g total fat
(1.5g sat. fat)
518mg sodium
10g carbs
<0.5g fiber
1g sugars
32g protein

---

boneless buffalo chicken wings

Pictured on pages 228–229

⅓ **cup panko bread crumbs**
⅛ **teaspoon garlic powder**
⅛ **teaspoon onion powder**
1 dash salt
1 dash black pepper
¼ **cup (about 2 large) egg whites or fat-free liquid egg substitute**
8 ounces raw boneless skinless chicken breast, cut into 10 nuggets
2 tablespoons Frank's RedHot Original Cayenne Pepper Sauce

1. In a wide bowl, mix bread crumbs with seasonings. Place egg whites/substitute in a second wide bowl. Coat chicken with egg, followed by the seasoned bread crumbs.

2. Spray an air fryer with nonstick spray. Place chicken nuggets in the air fryer, and spray with nonstick spray.

3. Set air fryer to 360°F. Cook until crispy and cooked through, about 12 minutes.

4. In a small bowl, combine hot sauce with 2 teaspoons water. Mix well.

5. Transfer chicken nuggets to a large bowl. Drizzle with sauce, and gently toss to coat.

MAKES 2 SERVINGS

190 calories

Prep: 10 minutes

Cook: 15 minutes

You'll Need: 2 wide bowls, air fryer, nonstick spray, small bowl, large bowl

½ of recipe (5 wings):
190 calories
3g total fat
(0.5g sat. fat)
781mg sodium
8g carbs
<0.5g fiber
0.5g sugars
29.5g protein

Honey Buffalo Chicken
Wings, page 230

Ranchy Chicken Nuggets,
page 226

Teriyaki Chicken Wings,
page 231

Boneless Buffalo
Chicken Wings,
page 227

Creamy
Sriracha
Chicken Wings,
page 232

honey buffalo chicken wings

Pictured on pages 228–229

2 tablespoons fat-free plain yogurt
2 tablespoons Frank's RedHot Original Cayenne Pepper Sauce, divided
1 tablespoon honey, divided
3 raw chicken wings, tips removed, drumettes and flats separated
½ teaspoon garlic powder

1. In a large sealable container, combine yogurt, 1 tablespoon hot sauce, and 1½ teaspoons honey. Add chicken wings, and toss to coat. Seal and marinate in the refrigerator for 1 hour.

2. Spray an air fryer with nonstick spray. Place wings in the air fryer, and discard excess marinade.

3. Set air fryer to 390°F. Cook until crispy and cooked through, 15–17 minutes.

4. To make the sauce, in a small bowl, combine remaining 1 tablespoon hot sauce, remaining 1½ teaspoons honey, garlic powder, and 2 teaspoons water. Mix well.

5. Place wings in a large bowl. Add sauce, and toss to coat.

MAKES 2 SERVINGS

232 calories

Prep: 10 minutes

Cook: 15 minutes

Marinate: 1 hour

You'll Need: large sealable container, air fryer, nonstick spray, small bowl, large bowl

½ of recipe (3 pieces):
232 calories
13g total fat
(3.5g sat. fat)
665mg sodium
10g carbs
0g fiber
9.5g sugars
18.5g protein

teriyaki chicken wings

Pictured on pages 228–229

3 tablespoons thick teriyaki sauce or marinade
2 teaspoons sweet chili sauce
½ teaspoon reduced-sodium soy sauce
3 raw chicken wings, tips removed, drumettes and flats separated
½ teaspoon sesame seeds
¼ teaspoon chopped garlic
1 tablespoon chopped scallions

1. In a small bowl, combine teriyaki sauce, chili sauce, and soy sauce. Mix well. Transfer half of the mixture to a large sealable bag or container, and set the remaining aside for later.

2. Add wings to the bag/container. Seal and marinate in the refrigerator for 1 hour.

3. Spray an air fryer with nonstick spray. Place wings in the air fryer, and discard excess marinade.

4. Set air fryer to 390°F. Cook until slightly crispy and cooked through, 15–17 minutes.

5. Place wings in a large bowl. Add remaining sauce, sesame seeds, and garlic. Toss to coat.

6. Top with scallions.

MAKES 2 SERVINGS

245 calories

Prep: 10 minutes

Cook: 20 minutes

Marinate: 1 hour

You'll Need: small bowl, large sealable bag or container, air fryer, nonstick spray, large bowl

½ of recipe (3 pieces):
245 calories
13g total fat
(3.5g sat. fat)
820mg sodium
11.5g carbs
<0.5g fiber
8g sugars
18g protein

creamy sriracha chicken wings

Pictured on pages 228–229

2 tablespoons light mayonnaise
2 tablespoons fat-free plain yogurt
1 tablespoon sriracha hot chili sauce
¼ teaspoon garlic powder
3 raw chicken wings, tips removed, drumettes and flats separated

1. In a small bowl, combine mayo, yogurt, chili sauce, and garlic powder. Mix well. Transfer half of the mixture to a large sealable bag or container, and set the remaining aside for later.

2. Add wings to the bag/container. Seal and marinate in the refrigerator for 1 hour.

3. Spray an air fryer with nonstick spray. Place wings in the air fryer, and discard excess marinade.

4. Set air fryer to 390°F. Cook until slightly crispy and cooked through, 15–17 minutes.

5. Place wings in a large bowl. Add remaining sauce mixture, and toss to coat.

MAKES 2 SERVINGS

250 calories

Prep: 10 minutes

Cook: 15 minutes

Marinate: 1 hour

You'll Need: small bowl, large sealable bag or container, air fryer, nonstick spray, large bowl

½ of recipe (3 pieces):
250 calories
17g total fat
(4g sat. fat)
432mg sodium
4.5g carbs
0g fiber
2g sugars
18g protein

loaded mashie egg rolls

Pictured on pages 236–237

8 ounces (about 1 medium) russet potato, peeled and cubed
½ cup chopped scallions
¼ cup shredded reduced-fat cheddar cheese
2 tablespoons precooked crumbled bacon
2 tablespoons whipped butter
2 tablespoons whipped cream cheese
2 tablespoons light sour cream
¼ teaspoon garlic powder
¼ teaspoon salt
⅛ teaspoon black pepper
6 egg roll wrappers

1. Bring a medium pot of water to a boil. Add potato, and cook until tender, 10–15 minutes.

2. Transfer potato to a large bowl. Add all remaining ingredients except egg roll wrappers. Thoroughly mash and mix.

3. Evenly distribute ⅙ of the filling (about ⅓ cup) along the center of an egg roll wrapper. Fold in the sides, and roll up the wrapper around the filling. Seal with a dab of water. Repeat to make five more egg rolls.

4. Spray an air fryer with nonstick spray. Place egg rolls in the air fryer, seam side down, and spray with nonstick spray.

5. Set air fryer to 390°F. Cook until golden brown, about 6 minutes.

MAKES 6 SERVINGS

150 calories

Prep: 10 minutes

Cook: 30 minutes

You'll Need: medium pot, potato masher, air fryer, nonstick spray

⅙ of recipe
(1 egg roll):
150 calories
5g total fat
(3g sat. fat)
350mg sodium
21.5g carbs
1g fiber
1.5g sugars
5.5g protein

burger blast egg rolls

Pictured on pages 236–237

8 ounces raw extra-lean ground beef (at least 95% lean)
2 tablespoons finely chopped onion
½ teaspoon garlic powder
½ teaspoon onion powder
⅛ teaspoon salt
⅛ teaspoon black pepper
¼ cup light Thousand Island dressing
1 tablespoon yellow mustard, or more for dipping
½ teaspoon white wine vinegar
½ cup shredded lettuce
¼ cup shredded reduced-fat cheddar cheese
6 hamburger dill pickle chips, chopped
1 tablespoon sesame seeds
6 egg roll wrappers
Optional dip: ketchup

1. Bring a skillet sprayed with nonstick spray to medium-high heat. Add beef, onion, and seasonings. Cook, stir, and crumble until beef is fully cooked and onion has softened, about 5 minutes.

2. Remove skillet from heat. Add dressing, mustard, and vinegar. Mix well.

3. Transfer beef mixture to a large bowl. Add lettuce, cheese, pickles, and sesame seeds. Mix thoroughly.

4. Evenly distribute ⅙ of the filling (about ⅓ cup) along the center of an egg roll wrapper. Fold in the sides, and roll up the wrapper around the filling. Seal with a dab of water. Repeat to make five more egg rolls.

5. Spray an air fryer with nonstick spray. Place egg rolls in the air fryer, seam side down, and spray with nonstick spray.

6. Set air fryer to 390°F. Cook until golden brown, about 6 minutes.

MAKES 6 SERVINGS

159 calories

30m

Prep: 15 minutes

Cook: 15 minutes

You'll Need: skillet, nonstick spray, large bowl, air fryer

**⅙ of recipe
(1 egg roll):**
159 calories
5g total fat
(1.5g sat. fat)
407mg sodium
16.5g carbs
1g fiber
2.5g sugars
11.5g protein

chicken pot pie egg rolls

Pictured on pages 236–237

⅓ cup chicken or turkey gravy

2 tablespoons whipped cream cheese

¼ teaspoon garlic powder

¼ teaspoon poultry seasoning

¼ teaspoon salt

1 cup frozen petite mixed vegetables, slightly thawed

6 ounces cooked and chopped skinless chicken breast

6 egg roll wrappers

1. In a large bowl, combine gravy, cream cheese, and seasonings. Mix until smooth and uniform. Add vegetables and chicken, and stir to coat.

2. Evenly distribute ⅙ of the filling (about ⅓ cup) along the center of an egg roll wrapper. Fold in the sides, and roll up the wrapper around the filling. Seal with a dab of water. Repeat to make five more egg rolls.

3. Spray an air fryer with nonstick spray. Place egg rolls in the air fryer, seam side down, and spray with nonstick spray.

4. Set air fryer to 390°F. Cook until golden brown, about 6 minutes.

MAKES 6 SERVINGS

130 calories

Prep: 10 minutes

Cook: 10 minutes

You'll Need: large bowl, air fryer, nonstick spray

**⅙ of recipe
(1 egg roll):**
130 calories
2g total fat
(0.5g sat. fat)
314mg sodium
16.5g carbs
1g fiber
1.5g sugars
11g protein

Lasagna Egg Rolls, page 239

Burger Blast
Egg Rolls,
page 234

**Chicken Pot Pie
Egg Rolls, page 235**

**Loaded Mashie
Egg Rolls, page 233**

**Philly Cheesesteak
Egg Rolls, page 238**

philly cheesesteak egg rolls

Pictured on pages 236–237

8 ounces raw extra-lean ground beef (at least 95% lean)
¼ teaspoon garlic powder
¼ teaspoon onion powder
¼ teaspoon salt
¼ teaspoon black pepper
¾ cup chopped green bell pepper
¾ cup chopped onion
2 slices reduced-fat provolone cheese, torn into pieces
3 tablespoons light/reduced-fat cream cheese
6 egg roll wrappers

1. Bring a large skillet sprayed with nonstick spray to medium-high heat. Add beef, and season with seasonings. Add bell pepper and onion. Cook, stir, and crumble until beef is fully cooked and veggies have softened, about 8 minutes.

2. Remove skillet from heat. Add provolone and cream cheese. Stir until thoroughly mixed and melted. Transfer to a large bowl.

3. Evenly distribute ⅙ of the filling (about ⅓ cup) along the center of an egg roll wrapper. Fold in the sides, and roll up the wrapper around the filling. Seal with a dab of water. Repeat to make five more egg rolls.

4. Spray an air fryer with nonstick spray. Place egg rolls in the air fryer, seam side down, and spray with nonstick spray.

5. Set air fryer to 390°F. Cook until golden brown, about 6 minutes.

MAKES 6 SERVINGS

157 calories

30m

Prep: 10 minutes

Cook: 15 minutes

You'll Need: large skillet, nonstick spray, large bowl, air fryer

⅙ of recipe
(1 egg roll):
157 calories
4.5g total fat
(2.5g sat. fat)
317mg sodium
16.5g carbs
1.5g fiber
2g sugars
12.5g protein

lasagna egg rolls

Pictured on pages 236–237

½ cup canned crushed tomatoes
3 tablespoons light/low-fat ricotta cheese
¾ teaspoon chopped garlic
¾ teaspoon onion powder
½ teaspoon Italian seasoning
1 dash ground nutmeg
2 dashes salt, divided
2 dashes black pepper, divided
4 ounces raw extra-lean ground beef (at least 95% lean)
2 tablespoons finely chopped onion
1½ cups roughly chopped spinach
¼ cup shredded part-skim mozzarella cheese
1 tablespoon finely chopped fresh basil
6 egg roll wrappers
Optional dip: additional crushed tomatoes with seasonings

1. In a medium bowl, combine crushed tomatoes, ricotta, garlic, onion powder, Italian seasoning, nutmeg, 1 dash salt, and 1 dash pepper. Mix until uniform.

2. Bring a skillet sprayed with nonstick spray to medium-high heat. Add beef, and season with remaining 1 dash salt and 1 dash pepper. Add onion, and cook and crumble until beef is fully cooked and onion has softened, about 4 minutes.

3. Reduce heat to medium low. Add tomato mixture and spinach. Cook and stir until spinach has wilted, about 1 minute.

4. Transfer mixture to a large bowl. Stir in mozzarella and basil.

5. Evenly distribute ⅙ of the filling (about ⅓ cup) along the center of an egg roll wrapper. Fold in the sides, and roll up the wrapper around the filling. Seal with a dab of water. Repeat to make 5 more egg rolls.

6. Spray an air fryer with nonstick spray. Place egg rolls in the air fryer, and spray with nonstick spray.

7. Set air fryer to 390°F. Cook until golden brown, about 6 minutes.

MAKES 6 SERVINGS

116 calories

30m

Prep: 10 minutes

Cook: 15 minutes

You'll Need: medium bowl, skillet, nonstick spray, large bowl, air fryer

⅙ of recipe (1 egg roll):
116 calories
2.5g total fat
(1g sat. fat)
263mg sodium
16g carbs
1g fiber
1.5g sugars
8.5g protein

HG FYI
Flip to page 223 for everything you ever wanted to know about egg roll wrappers!

cheesy chicken taquitos

Pictured on pages 242–243

2½ tablespoons taco sauce
2 tablespoons whipped cream cheese
⅛ teaspoon garlic powder
4 ounces cooked and shredded skinless chicken breast
Four 6-inch corn tortillas

1. In a medium bowl, combine taco sauce, cream cheese, and garlic powder. Mix until smooth and uniform. Stir in chicken.

2. Place tortillas between 2 damp paper towels. Microwave for 30 seconds, or until warm and pliable.

3. Spread one tortilla with ¼ of the chicken mixture, about 3 tablespoons. Tightly roll up into a tube, and secure with a toothpick. Repeat to make three more taquitos.

4. Spray an air fryer with nonstick spray. Place taquitos in the air fryer, seam side down, and spray with nonstick spray.

5. Set air fryer to 370°F. Cook until crispy and golden brown, about 8 minutes.

MAKES 2 SERVINGS

224 calories

  GF

Prep: 10 minutes

Cook: 15 minutes

You'll Need: medium bowl, air fryer, nonstick spray

**½ of recipe
(2 taquitos):**
224 calories
5.5g total fat
(2g sat. fat)
264mg sodium
23g carbs
2g fiber
1.5g sugars
19.5g protein

cheesy beef empanadas

Pictured on pages 242–243

½ cup self-rising flour
½ cup fat-free plain Greek yogurt
3 ounces raw extra-lean ground beef (at least 95% lean)
⅛ teaspoon garlic powder
⅛ teaspoon onion powder
1 dash salt
1 dash black pepper
¼ cup shredded reduced-fat Mexican-blend cheese
2 tablespoons light/reduced-fat cream cheese

1. In a large bowl, mix flour and yogurt until dough forms.

2. Bring a skillet sprayed with nonstick spray to medium-high heat. Add beef, garlic powder, onion powder, salt, and pepper. Cook and crumble until fully cooked, about 2 minutes.

3. Remove skillet from heat, and stir in shredded cheese and cream cheese.

4. Shape dough into two circles, each about 6 inches in diameter and ¼ inch thick. Top half of each circle with seasoned beef.

5. Fold the top half of each circle over the filling so the top edge meets the bottom. Firmly press edges with a fork to seal.

6. Spray an air fryer with nonstick spray. Place empanadas in the air fryer, and spray with nonstick spray.

7. Set air fryer to 360°F. Cook until tops are light golden brown and dough is cooked through, about 10 minutes.

MAKES 2 SERVINGS

275 calories

5i **30m**

Prep: 10 minutes

Cook: 15 minutes

You'll Need: large bowl, skillet, nonstick spray, air fryer

**½ of recipe
(1 empanada):**
275 calories
8.5g total fat
(5g sat. fat)
702mg sodium
26g carbs
1g fiber
3g sugars
23.5g protein

Cheesy Beef Empanadas,
page 241

Cheesy Chicken Taquitos,
page 240

Southwest Chicken Empanadas,
page 244

southwest chicken empanadas

Pictured on pages 242–243

½ cup self-rising flour
½ cup fat-free plain Greek yogurt
3 ounces cooked and chopped skinless chicken breast
¼ cup shredded reduced-fat Mexican-blend cheese
2 tablespoons chopped cilantro
2 tablespoons frozen sweet corn kernels, thawed
2 tablespoons chopped red onion
1 tablespoon taco sauce
1½ teaspoons taco seasoning

1. In a large bowl, mix flour and yogurt until dough forms.

2. In a medium bowl, combine chicken, cheese, cilantro, corn, onion, taco sauce, and taco seasoning. Mix well.

3. Shape dough into two circles, each about 6 inches in diameter and ¼ inch thick. Top half of each circle with chicken mixture.

4. Fold the top half of each circle over the filling so the top edge meets the bottom. Firmly press edges with a fork to seal.

5. Spray an air fryer with nonstick spray. Place empanadas in the air fryer, and spray with nonstick spray.

6. Set air fryer to 360°F. Cook until tops are light golden brown and dough is cooked through, about 10 minutes.

MAKES 2 SERVINGS

279 calories

 30m

Prep: 15 minutes

Cook: 10 minutes

You'll Need: large bowl, medium bowl, air fryer, nonstick spray

½ of recipe (1 empanada):
279 calories
5.5g total fat
(2.5g sat. fat)
742mg sodium
30g carbs
2g fiber
3.5g sugars
27g protein

burgers, wraps & sandwiches

creamy jalapeño stuffed burgers

Pictured on pages 248–249

2 tablespoons light/reduced-fat cream cheese
1 tablespoon canned diced jalapeño peppers, drained
1 teaspoon dried minced onion
¼ teaspoon garlic powder, divided
¼ teaspoon onion powder, divided
8 ounces raw extra-lean ground beef (at least 95% lean)
¼ teaspoon salt
¼ teaspoon black pepper
Optional topping: sliced jalapeño peppers

1. In a medium bowl, combine cream cheese, jalapeño peppers, minced onion, ⅛ teaspoon garlic powder, and ⅛ teaspoon onion powder. Mix until uniform.

2. In a large bowl, combine beef, salt, pepper, remaining ⅛ teaspoon garlic powder, and remaining ⅛ teaspoon onion powder. Mix thoroughly.

3. Form beef into four thin patties. Divide cream cheese mixture among two patties. Top each with another patty. Squeeze the top and bottom patties' edges together to seal, forming two stuffed patties.

4. Spray an air fryer with nonstick spray. Place patties in the air fryer.

5. Set to 390°F. Cook for about 12 minutes, until cooked through.

MAKES 2 SERVINGS

186 calories

Prep: 10 minutes

Cook: 15 minutes

You'll Need: medium bowl, large bowl, air fryer, nonstick spray

½ of recipe (1 patty):
186 calories
7.5g total fat
(4g sat. fat)
480mg sodium
3g carbs
0.5g fiber
1g sugars
25g protein

hawaiian stuffed burgers

Pictured on pages 248–249

2 tablespoons light/reduced-fat cream cheese
1 tablespoon crushed pineapple packed in juice, drained
½ ounce (about 1 slice) reduced-sodium ham, roughly chopped
8 ounces raw extra-lean ground beef (at least 95% lean)
¼ teaspoon garlic powder
¼ teaspoon onion powder
¼ teaspoon salt
¼ teaspoon black pepper
Optional topping: grilled pineapple

1. In a small bowl, mix cream cheese and pineapple. Stir in chopped ham.

2. In a large bowl, combine beef and seasonings. Mix thoroughly.

3. Form beef into four thin patties. Divide cream cheese mixture among two patties. Top each with another patty. Squeeze the top and bottom patties' edges together to seal, forming two stuffed patties.

4. Spray an air fryer with nonstick spray. Place patties in the air fryer.

5. Set air fryer to 390°F. Cook for about 12 minutes, until cooked through.

MAKES 2 SERVINGS

193 calories

Prep: 10 minutes

Cook: 15 minutes

You'll Need: small bowl, large bowl, air fryer, nonstick spray

½ of recipe (1 patty):
193 calories
8g total fat
(4g sat. fat)
497mg sodium
3g carbs
<0.5g fiber
2g sugars
26g protein

bacon & blue cheese stuffed burgers

Pictured on pages 248–249

2 tablespoons crumbled blue cheese, or more for topping
2 tablespoons light/reduced-fat cream cheese
2 teaspoons precooked crumbled bacon
8 ounces raw extra-lean ground beef (at least 95% lean)
¼ teaspoon garlic powder
¼ teaspoon onion powder
¼ teaspoon salt
¼ teaspoon black pepper

1. In a small bowl, mix blue cheese and cream cheese. Stir in bacon.

2. In a large bowl, combine beef and seasonings. Mix thoroughly.

3. Form beef into four thin patties. Divide cheese mixture among two patties. Top each with another patty. Squeeze the top and bottom patties' edges together to seal, forming two stuffed patties.

4. Spray an air fryer with nonstick spray. Place patties in the air fryer.

5. Set air fryer to 390°F. Cook for about 12 minutes, until cooked through.

MAKES 2 SERVINGS

217 calories

Prep: 10 minutes

Cook: 15 minutes

You'll Need: small bowl, large bowl, air fryer, nonstick spray

½ of recipe (1 patty):
217 calories
10g total fat
(5.5g sat. fat)
597mg sodium
2g carbs
<0.5g fiber
1g sugars
27g protein

Hawaiian Stuffed
Burgers, page 246

Pepperoni Pizza Stuffed
Burgers, page 250

Black Bean
Burgers,
page 251

Bacon & Blue Cheese
Stuffed Burgers,
page 247

Creamy Jalapeño
Stuffed Burgers,
page 245

pepperoni pizza stuffed burgers

Pictured on pages 248–249

1½ tablespoons marinara sauce with 70 calories or less per ½-cup serving
1 tablespoons shredded part-skim mozzarella cheese
½ tablespoon grated Parmesan cheese
4 pieces turkey pepperoni, chopped
8 ounces raw extra-lean ground beef (at least 95% lean)
¼ teaspoon garlic powder
¼ teaspoon Italian seasoning
¼ teaspoon onion powder
¼ teaspoon salt
¼ teaspoon black pepper

1. In a small bowl, combine marinara, mozzarella, and Parm. Mix thoroughly. Stir in chopped pepperoni.

2. In a large bowl, combine beef and seasonings. Mix thoroughly.

3. Form beef into four thin patties. Divide cheese mixture among two patties. Top each with another patty. Squeeze the top and bottom patties' edges together to seal, forming two stuffed patties.

4. Spray an air fryer with nonstick spray. Place patties in the air fryer.

5. Set air fryer to 390°F. Cook for about 12 minutes, until cooked through.

MAKES 2 SERVINGS

183 calories

Prep: 10 minutes

Cook: 15 minutes

You'll Need: small bowl, large bowl, air fryer, nonstick spray

½ of recipe
(1 patty):
183 calories
6.5g total fat
(3g sat. fat)
601mg sodium
2g carbs
0.5g fiber
1g sugars
27g protein

black bean burgers

Pictured on pages 248–249

1 cup canned black beans, drained and rinsed

2 tablespoons (about 1 large) egg whites or fat-free liquid egg substitute

1 teaspoon chopped garlic

⅓ cup panko bread crumbs

⅓ cup seeded and chopped tomato

¼ cup chopped fresh cilantro

2 tablespoons canned diced jalapeño peppers, drained

⅛ teaspoon salt

1. In a medium bowl, combine beans, egg white/substitute, and garlic. Thoroughly mash with a potato masher.

2. Add all remaining ingredients. Mix until uniform.

3. Form mixture into 2 patties.

4. Spray an air fryer with nonstick spray. Place burgers in the air fryer.

5. Set air fryer to 375°F. Cook until lightly browned, about 10 minutes, flipping halfway through.

MAKES 2 SERVINGS

163 calories

Prep: 10 minutes

Cook: 10 minutes

You'll Need: medium bowl, air fryer, nonstick spray

½ of recipe (1 patty):
163 calories
1g total fat
(0g sat. fat)
601mg sodium
29g carbs
6.5g fiber
2.5g sugars
9.5g protein

lettuce-wrapped burger sliders

8 ounces raw extra-lean ground beef (at least 95% lean)
¼ cup finely chopped onion
¼ teaspoon garlic powder
¼ teaspoon onion powder
⅛ teaspoon salt
⅛ teaspoon black pepper
2 slices reduced-fat cheddar cheese, each cut into 3 strips
6 medium iceberg or butter lettuce leaves
Optional dips/toppings: ketchup, yellow mustard, pickles

1. In a large bowl, combine beef and seasonings. Mix thoroughly.

2. Form beef into 6 small patties.

3. Spray an air fryer with nonstick spray. Place patties in the air fryer.

4. Set air fryer to 390°F. Cook for 10 minutes, until cooked through.

5. Immediately top patties with cheese. Wrap each patty in a lettuce leaf.

MAKES 2 SERVINGS

233 calories

Prep: 10 minutes

Cook: 10 minutes

You'll Need: large bowl, air fryer, nonstick spray

½ of recipe (3 sliders):
233 calories
10g total fat
(5g sat. fat)
363mg sodium
5g carbs
1.5g fiber
2.5g sugars
31g protein

turkey reuben wrap

Pictured on pages 258–259

2 tablespoons sauerkraut, blotted dry
1 teaspoon yellow mustard
1 low-carb flour tortilla with 100 calories or less
1½ ounces (about 3 slices) reduced-sodium skinless turkey breast
1 slice reduced-fat Swiss cheese

1. In a small bowl, mix sauerkraut and mustard until uniform.

2. Spread mixture along the center of the tortilla, and top with turkey and cheese. Wrap tortilla up like a burrito: Fold in the sides, and then roll it up from the bottom.

3. Spray an air fryer with nonstick spray. Place wrap in the air fryer, seam side down.

4. Set air fryer to 375°F. Cook until golden brown and crispy, about 5 minutes.

MAKES 1 SERVING

218 calories

Prep: 5 minutes

Cook: 5 minutes

You'll Need: small bowl, air fryer, nonstick spray

Entire recipe:
218 calories
8g total fat
(3.5g sat. fat)
819mg sodium
21g carbs
8.5g fiber
1g sugars
21.5g protein

hawaiian BBQ chicken wrap

Pictured on pages 258–259

1 tablespoon chopped fresh cilantro
1 tablespoon light/reduced-fat cream cheese
1 tablespoon chopped red onion
1 tablespoon canned crushed pineapple packed in juice, drained
2 ounces cooked and shredded skinless chicken breast
1 tablespoon BBQ sauce
1 low-carb flour tortilla with 100 calories or less

1. In a small bowl, combine cilantro, cream cheese, onion, and pineapple. Mix well.

2. In another small bowl, coat chicken with BBQ sauce.

3. Spread cheese mixture along the center of the tortilla, and top with BBQ chicken. Wrap tortilla up like a burrito: Fold in the sides, and then roll it up from the bottom.

4. Spray an air fryer with nonstick spray. Place wrap in the air fryer, seam side down.

5. Set air fryer to 375°F. Cook until golden brown and crispy, about 5 minutes.

MAKES 1 SERVING

268 calories

15m

Prep: 5 minutes

Cook: 5 minutes

You'll Need: 2 small bowls, air fryer, nonstick spray

Entire recipe:
268 calories
8g total fat
(3.5g sat. fat)
505mg sodium
30.5g carbs
7.5g fiber
9.5g sugars
22.5g protein

cheesy hot tuna wrap

Pictured on pages 258–259

1 tablespoon light mayonnaise

½ teaspoon Dijon mustard

¼ teaspoon garlic powder

¼ teaspoon onion powder

One 2.6-ounce packet albacore tuna packed in water, drained
and flaked

¼ cup finely chopped onion

1 low-carb flour tortilla with 100 calories or less

1 slice reduced-fat cheddar cheese

1. In a medium bowl, combine mayo, mustard, garlic powder, and onion powder. Mix well. Add tuna and onion, and stir to coat.

2. Spread mixture along the center of the tortilla, and top with cheese. Wrap tortilla up like a burrito: Fold in the sides, and then roll it up from the bottom.

3. Spray an air fryer with nonstick spray. Place wrap in the air fryer, seam side down.

4. Set air fryer to 375°F. Cook until golden brown and crispy, about 5 minutes.

MAKES 1 SERVING

313 calories

Prep: 5 minutes

Cook: 5 minutes

You'll Need: medium bowl, air fryer, nonstick spray

Entire recipe:
313 calories
13.5g total fat
(5g sat. fat)
761mg sodium
25.5g carbs
8g fiber
3g sugars
26.5g protein

white pizza wrap

Pictured on pages 258–259

⅓ cup shredded part-skim mozzarella cheese
3 tablespoons light/low-fat ricotta cheese
1 tablespoon chopped fresh basil
1 tablespoon whipped cream cheese
2 teaspoons grated Parmesan cheese
¼ teaspoon garlic powder
1 low-carb flour tortilla with 100 calories or less

1. In a medium bowl, combine mozzarella, ricotta, basil, cream cheese, Parm, and garlic powder. Mix until uniform.

2. Spread mixture along the center of the tortilla. Wrap tortilla up like a burrito: Fold in the sides, and then roll it up from the bottom.

3. Spray an air fryer with nonstick spray. Place wrap in an air fryer, seam side down.

4. Set air fryer to 375°F. Cook until golden brown and crispy, about 5 minutes.

MAKES 1 SERVING

307 calories

 15m

Prep: 5 minutes

Cook: 5 minutes

You'll Need: medium bowl, air fryer, nonstick spray

Entire recipe:
307 calories
16g total fat
(9.5g sat. fat)
710mg sodium
24.5g carbs
8g fiber
3.5g sugars
21.5g protein

Easy Grilled Cheese,
page 261

Toasted Chicken Fajita
Wrap, page 260

Turkey Reuben Wrap, page 254

Cheesy Hot Tuna Wrap, page 256

White Pizza Wrap, page 257

Hawaiian BBQ Chicken Wrap, page 255

Cuban Sandwich Pockets, page 262

toasted chicken fajita wrap

Pictured on pages 258–259

2 ounces raw boneless skinless chicken breast, cut into bite-sized pieces
¼ cup thinly sliced bell pepper
¼ cup thinly sliced onion
½ teaspoon fajita seasoning
2 tablespoons canned black beans, drained and rinsed
2 tablespoons shredded reduced-fat Mexican-blend cheese
1 low-carb flour tortilla with 100 calories or less

1. Bring a skillet sprayed with nonstick spray to medium-high heat. Add chicken, pepper, onion, and fajita seasoning. Cook and stir until veggies are tender and chicken is fully cooked, about 5 minutes.

2. Remove skillet from heat. Stir in black beans.

3. Place mixture along the center of the tortilla, and top with cheese. Wrap tortilla up like a burrito: Fold in the sides, and then roll it up from the bottom.

4. Spray an air fryer with nonstick spray. Place wrap in the air fryer, seam side down.

5. Set air fryer to 375°F. Cook until golden brown and crispy, about 5 minutes.

MAKES 1 SERVING

257 calories

15m

Prep: 5 minutes

Cook: 10 minutes

You'll Need: skillet, nonstick spray, air fryer

Entire recipe:
257 calories
7.5g total fat
(3.5g sat. fat)
556mg sodium
29g carbs
10g fiber
3g sugars
23g protein

easy grilled cheese

Pictured on pages 258–259

1 teaspoon whipped butter
2 slices whole-grain bread with 60–80 calories per slice
⅛ teaspoon garlic powder
⅛ teaspoon onion powder
1 slice reduced-fat cheddar cheese

1. Spread butter onto bread. Top with seasonings.

2. Spray an air fryer with nonstick spray. Place one slice of bread in the air fryer, buttered side down. Top with cheddar and the other slice of bread, buttered side up.

3. Set air fryer to 360°F. Cook until golden brown and melty, 8–10 minutes, flipping halfway through.

MAKES 1 SERVING

223 calories

Prep: 5 minutes

Cook: 10 minutes

You'll Need: air fryer, nonstick spray

Entire recipe:
223 calories
8.5g total fat
(4g sat. fat)
375mg sodium
27.5g carbs
5g fiber
3.5g sugars
11.5g protein

cuban sandwich pockets

Pictured on pages 258–259

½ cup self-rising flour
½ cup fat-free plain Greek yogurt
1 slice reduced-fat Swiss cheese, halved
1½ ounces (about 2 slices) reduced-sodium ham, roughly chopped
2 teaspoons mustard
2 tablespoons chopped dill pickles

1. In a medium bowl, mix flour and yogurt until dough forms.

2. Shape dough into two squares, each about 6 inches by 6 inches and ¼ inch thick. Top half of each square with cheese, chopped ham, mustard, and pickles.

3. Fold the top half of each square over the filling so the top edge meets the bottom. Firmly press edges with a fork to seal.

4. Spray an air fryer with nonstick spray. Place pockets in the air fryer, and spray with nonstick spray.

5. Set air fryer to 360°F. Cook until golden brown and cooked through, about 10 minutes.

MAKES 2 SERVINGS

195 calories

 30m

Prep: 10 minutes

Cook: 15 minutes

You'll Need: medium bowl, air fryer, nonstick spray

½ of recipe (1 pocket):
195 calories
2.5g total fat
(1g sat. fat)
760mg sodium
26.5g carbs
1g fiber
3g sugars
16g protein

pizzas & calzones

sausage ricotta pizza

Pictured on pages 264–265

⅓ cup light/low-fat ricotta cheese

1 tablespoon shredded part-skim mozzarella cheese

¼ teaspoon chopped garlic

¼ cup self-rising flour

¼ teaspoon Italian seasoning

¼ cup fat-free plain Greek yogurt

1½ ounces (about ½ link) fully cooked chicken sausage, chopped

1½ teaspoons fresh basil

1. In a small bowl, combine ricotta, mozzarella, and garlic. Mix thoroughly.

2. Cut heavy-duty aluminum foil into a piece a few inches smaller than your air fryer basket. Spray with nonstick spray.

3. In a large bowl, mix flour and Italian seasoning. Add yogurt, and mix until dough forms.

4. Shape dough into a circle about 6 inches in diameter and ¼ inch thick.

5. Place dough on the foil. Spread with cheese mixture, leaving a ½-inch border. Top with chopped sausage.

6. Transfer pizza on the foil into an air fryer. Set air fryer to 360°F. Cook until cheese has melted and crust is crispy, about 10 minutes.

7. Top with basil.

MAKES 1 SERVING

299 calories

30m

Prep: 10 minutes

Cook: 10 minutes

You'll Need: small bowl, heavy-duty aluminum foil, nonstick spray, air fryer

Entire recipe:
299 calories
8g total fat
(4g sat. fat)
778mg sodium
30.5g carbs
0.5g fiber
7g sugars
25g protein

BBQ Chicken Pizza,
page 266

Elote-Topped Pizza,
page 267

Sausage Ricotta Pizza,
page 263

BBQ chicken pizza

Pictured on pages 264–265

2 ounces cooked and chopped skinless chicken breast
⅛ teaspoon garlic powder
⅛ teaspoon onion powder
1½ tablespoons BBQ sauce, divided
¼ cup self-rising flour
¼ teaspoon Italian seasoning
¼ cup fat-free plain Greek yogurt
1 tablespoon finely chopped red onion
3 tablespoons shredded part-skim mozzarella cheese
1 tablespoon finely chopped fresh cilantro

1. In a small bowl, combine chicken, garlic powder, onion powder, and 1½ teaspoons BBQ sauce. Mix well.

2. Cut heavy-duty aluminum foil into a piece a few inches smaller than your air fryer basket. Spray with nonstick spray.

3. In a large bowl, mix flour and Italian seasoning. Add yogurt. Mix until dough forms.

4. Shape dough into a circle about 6 inches in diameter and ¼ inch thick.

5. Place dough on the foil. Spread with remaining 1 tablespoon BBQ sauce, leaving a ½-inch border. Top with chicken, onion, and cheese.

6. Transfer pizza on the foil into an air fryer. Set air fryer to 360°F. Cook until cheese has melted and crust is crispy, 7–8 minutes.

7. Top with cilantro.

MAKES 1 SERVING

330 calories

Prep: 10 minutes

Cook: 10 minutes

You'll Need: small bowl, heavy-duty aluminum foil, nonstick spray, large bowl, air fryer

Entire recipe:
330 calories
6g total fat
(3g sat. fat)
771mg sodium
35.5g carbs
0g fiber
11.5g sugars
31g protein

elote-topped pizza

Pictured on pages 264–265

¼ cup frozen sweet corn kernels

1 dash ground cumin

1 dash chili powder

2 tablespoons light mayonnaise

1 tablespoon crumbled feta cheese

1 tablespoon chopped fresh cilantro, divided

⅛ teaspoon garlic powder

2 tablespoons cornmeal

2 tablespoons self-rising flour

¼ teaspoon Italian seasoning

¼ cup fat-free plain Greek yogurt

2 tablespoons shredded part-skim mozzarella cheese

1. Bring a skillet sprayed with nonstick spray to medium-high heat. Add corn, cumin, and chili powder. Cook and stir until blackened, about 4 minutes.

2. Transfer corn to a small bowl. Add mayo, feta, 1½ teaspoons cilantro, and garlic powder. Mix thoroughly.

3. Cut heavy-duty aluminum foil into a piece a few inches smaller than your air fryer basket. Spray with nonstick spray.

4. In a large bowl, combine cornmeal, flour, and Italian seasoning. Mix well. Add yogurt. Mix until dough forms.

5. Shape dough into a circle about 6 inches in diameter and ¼ inch thick.

6. Place dough on the foil. Top with corn mixture, leaving a ½-inch border. Top with cheese.

7. Transfer pizza on the foil into an air fryer. Set air fryer to 360°F. Cook until cheese has melted and crust is crispy, about 10 minutes.

8. Top with remaining 1½ teaspoons cilantro.

MAKES 1 SERVING

320 calories

Prep: 10 minutes

Cook: 15 minutes

You'll Need: skillet, nonstick spray, small bowl, heavy-duty aluminum foil, large bowl, air fryer

Entire recipe:
320 calories
12.5g total fat
(2.5g sat. fat)
607mg sodium
36.5g carbs
1.5g fiber
4.5g sugars
14.5g protein

Sausage & Bell Pepper Calzones, page 270

Italian Ham & Cheese Calzones, opposite page

italian ham & cheese calzones

Pictured on opposite page

⅓ **cup light/low-fat ricotta cheese**

¼ **cup shredded part-skim mozzarella cheese**

¼ **teaspoon chopped garlic**

½ **cup self-rising flour**

½ **cup fat-free plain Greek yogurt**

1½ **ounces (about 2 slices) reduced-sodium ham, roughly chopped**

1. In a small bowl, combine ricotta, mozzarella, and garlic. Mix well.

2. In a large bowl, mix flour and yogurt until dough forms.

3. Shape dough into two circles, each about 6 inches in diameter and ¼ thick. Spread cheese mixture over half of each circle, leaving a ½-inch border. Top with chopped ham.

4. Fold the top half of each circle over the filling so the top edge meets the bottom. Firmly press edges with a fork to seal.

5. Spray an air fryer with nonstick spray. Place calzones in the air fryer, and spray with nonstick spray.

6. Set air fryer to 360°F. Cook until tops are light golden brown and dough is cooked through, about 10 minutes.

MAKES 2 SERVINGS

233 calories

30m

Prep: 10 minutes

Cook: 10 minutes

You'll Need: small bowl, large bowl, air fryer, nonstick spray

½ of recipe (1 calzone):
233 calories
4.5g total fat
(3g sat. fat)
693mg sodium
28g carbs
1g fiber
4.5g sugars
20g protein

sausage & bell pepper calzones

Pictured on page 268

½ cup sliced bell pepper
3 ounces (about 1 link) fully cooked chicken sausage, sliced into coins
¼ cup marinara sauce with 70 calories or less per ½-cup serving
½ cup self-rising flour
½ cup fat-free plain Greek yogurt
¼ cup shredded part-skim mozzarella cheese

1. Bring a skillet sprayed with nonstick spray to medium-high heat. Add pepper, and cook and stir until slightly softened and lightly browned, about 3 minutes. Add sausage, and cook and stir until browned, about 2 minutes.

2. Remove skillet from heat. Stir in marinara.

3. In a large bowl, mix flour and yogurt until dough forms.

4. Shape dough into two circles, each about 6 inches in diameter and ¼ inch thick. Top half of each circle with the sausage mixture and mozzarella.

5. Fold the top half of each circle over the filling so the top edge meets the bottom. Firmly press edges with a fork to seal.

6. Spray an air fryer with nonstick spray. Place calzones in the air fryer, and spray with nonstick spray.

7. Set air fryer to 360°F. Cook until tops are light golden brown and dough is cooked through, about 10 minutes.

MAKES 2 SERVINGS

261 calories

30m

Prep: 10 minutes

Cook: 15 minutes

You'll Need: skillet, nonstick spray, large bowl, air fryer

½ of recipe (1 calzone):
261 calories
7g total fat
(2.5g sat. fat)
823mg sodium
29g carbs
2g fiber
4.5g sugars
20g protein

HG FYI
These pizzas and calzones are made with our miraculous 2-ingredient dough. For more of these dough-licious recipes—plus helpful tips & tricks—flip to page 187.

BBQ meatless meatloaf

Pictured on page 272

1 cup chopped mushrooms
1 cup finely chopped onion
2 teaspoons chopped garlic
3 cups meatless crumbles (refrigerated or slightly thawed from frozen)
¾ cup panko bread crumbs
½ cup (about 4 large) egg whites or fat-free liquid egg substitute
1 teaspoon ground cumin
1 teaspoon onion powder
2 tablespoons BBQ sauce
2 tablespoons ketchup

1. Cut a piece of heavy-duty aluminum foil into a square about the size of your air fryer basket. Spray with nonstick spray.

2. Bring a skillet sprayed with nonstick spray to medium-high heat. Add mushrooms, onion, and garlic. Cook and stir until mostly softened and lightly browned, about 4 minutes.

3. Transfer mixture to a large bowl. Add all remaining ingredients except BBQ sauce and ketchup. Mix thoroughly.

4. Form mixture into a loaf on the foil. Place in an air fryer.

5. In a small bowl, mix BBQ sauce with ketchup. Spread over meatloaf.

6. Set air fryer to 360°F. Cook until firm with lightly browned edges, 30–35 minutes.

MAKES 5 SERVINGS

161 calories

Prep: 10 minutes

Cook: 35 minutes

You'll Need: heavy-duty aluminum foil, skillet, nonstick spray, large bowl, air fryer, small bowl

⅕ of recipe:
161 calories
2g total fat
(0g sat. fat)
423mg sodium
23g carbs
5g fiber
6.5g sugars
16.5g protein

Honey BBQ
Meatloaf,
opposite page

BBQ Meatless
Meatloaf,
page 271

honey BBQ meatloaf

Pictured on opposite page

¼ cup **BBQ sauce**

2 tablespoons **honey**

1 pound **raw extra-lean ground beef (at least 95% lean)**

1 cup **chopped onion**

½ cup **panko bread crumbs**

¼ cup **(about 2 large) egg whites or fat-free liquid egg substitute**

½ teaspoon **garlic powder**

½ teaspoon **onion powder**

⅛ teaspoon **salt**

⅛ teaspoon **black pepper**

1. Cut a piece of heavy-duty aluminum foil into a square about the size of your air fryer basket. Spray with nonstick spray.

2. In a small bowl, mix BBQ sauce with honey.

3. In a large bowl, combine remaining ingredients. Add half of the honey BBQ mixture, and mix thoroughly.

4. Form meat into a loaf on the foil. Place in an air fryer. Top with remaining honey BBQ mixture.

5. Set air fryer to 360°F. Cook for 30–35 minutes, until cooked through.

MAKES 5 SERVINGS

195 calories

Prep: 10 minutes

Cook: 35 minutes

You'll Need: heavy-duty aluminum foil, nonstick spray, small bowl, large bowl, air fryer

⅕ of recipe:
195 calories
4g total fat
(1.5g sat. fat)
270mg sodium
17g carbs
0.5g fiber
10g sugars
21g protein

stuffed chicken parm

Pictured on opposite page

¼ cup panko bread crumbs
½ teaspoon Italian seasoning, divided
½ teaspoon garlic powder, divided
½ teaspoon onion powder, divided
Two 5-ounce raw boneless skinless chicken breast cutlets, pounded to
    ½-inch thickness
⅛ teaspoon salt
⅛ teaspoon black pepper
3 tablespoons shredded part-skim mozzarella cheese
¼ cup (about 2 large) egg whites or fat-free liquid egg substitute
¼ cup marinara sauce with 70 calories or less per ½-cup serving
2 teaspoons grated Parmesan cheese

270 calories

Prep: 15 minutes

Cook: 25 minutes

You'll Need: medium bowl, wide bowl, air fryer, nonstick spray, small microwave-safe bowl

½ of recipe (1 stuffed chicken breast):
270 calories
7g total fat
(2.5g sat. fat)
476mg sodium
10g carbs
1g fiber
2.5g sugars
39g protein

1. In a medium bowl, combine bread crumbs, ¼ teaspoon Italian seasoning, ¼ teaspoon garlic powder, and ¼ teaspoon onion powder. Mix well.

2. Season chicken with salt, pepper, and remaining ¼ teaspoon Italian seasoning, ¼ teaspoon garlic powder, and ¼ teaspoon onion powder. Top with mozzarella. Tightly roll up each chicken cutlet, and secure with toothpicks.

3. Place one stuffed chicken cutlet in a wide bowl. Top with half of the egg whites/substitute. Coat the top half of the chicken with half of the seasoned breadcrumbs. Repeat with remaining stuffed chicken cutlet.

4. Spray an air fryer with nonstick spray. Place stuffed chicken cutlets in the air fryer, and spray with nonstick spray.

5. Set air fryer to 365°F. Cook until crispy and cooked through, 20–25 minutes.

6. Place marinara in a small microwave-safe bowl. Cover and microwave for 20 seconds, or until hot.

7. Top chicken with marinara and Parm.

MAKES 2 SERVINGS

Elote-Topped Crispy Chicken,
page 286

Stuffed
Chicken Parm,
opposite page

BBQ chicken tenders with almond-apple slaw

Slaw

1 tablespoon light mayonnaise
1 teaspoon seasoned rice vinegar
2 cups bagged coleslaw mix
¼ ounce (about 1 tablespoon) sliced almonds
¼ cup chopped apple
Optional: salt and black pepper

Chicken

⅓ cup panko bread crumbs
1 teaspoon garlic powder
1 teaspoon onion powder
⅛ teaspoon salt
⅛ teaspoon black pepper
3 tablespoons BBQ sauce, or more for dipping
10 ounces raw boneless skinless chicken breast, cut into 10 strips

1. In a medium bowl, mix mayo with vinegar. Add coleslaw mix, and stir to coat. Mix in almonds and apple. Optional: Add salt and pepper to taste.

2. In a wide bowl, mix bread crumbs with seasonings. Place BBQ sauce in a second wide bowl. Coat chicken with BBQ sauce, followed by the seasoned bread crumbs.

3. Spray an air fryer with nonstick spray. Place chicken strips in the air fryer, and spray with nonstick spray.

4. Set air fryer to 360°F. Cook until crispy and cooked through, about 12 minutes.

MAKES 2 SERVINGS

327 calories

30m

Prep: 10 minutes

Cook: 15 minutes

You'll Need: medium bowl, 2 wide bowls, air fryer, nonstick spray

½ of recipe (5 tenders with about 1 cup slaw):
327 calories
7.5g total fat
(1g sat. fat)
502mg sodium
27.5g carbs
2.5g fiber
14.5g sugars
34.5g protein

crunchy coconut chicken strips with spicy mayo and coleslaw

Slaw

2 cups bagged coleslaw mix
1 tablespoon finely chopped fresh cilantro
1 tablespoon seasoned rice vinegar

Chicken

¼ cup panko bread crumbs
3 tablespoons unsweetened shredded coconut
1 packet natural no-calorie sweetener
¼ teaspoon chili powder
⅛ teaspoon garlic powder
¼ cup (about 2 large) egg white or fat-free liquid egg substitute
⅛ teaspoon coconut extract
8 ounces raw boneless skinless chicken breast, cut into 8 strips

Sauce

2 tablespoons sweet chili sauce
2 tablespoons light mayonnaise
2 teaspoons sriracha chili sauce

343 calories

30m

Prep: 10 minutes

Cook: 20 minutes

You'll Need: medium bowl, 2 wide bowls, air fryer, nonstick spray, small bowl

½ of recipe (4 strips with about 1 cup slaw):
343 calories
10.5g total fat
(4g sat. fat)
847mg sodium
30g carbs
3.5g fiber
17g sugars
29g protein

1. In a medium bowl, combine slaw ingredients. Mix well. Cover and refrigerate until ready to serve.

2. In a wide bowl, combine bread crumbs, shredded coconut, sweetener, and seasonings. Mix well.

3. In a second wide bowl, mix egg whites/substitute with coconut extract. Coat chicken with egg mixture, followed by the seasoned bread crumbs.

4. Spray an air fryer with nonstick spray. Place chicken strips in the air fryer, and spray with nonstick spray.

5. Set air fryer to 360°F. Cook until crispy and cooked through, about 16 minutes.

6. In a small bowl, combine sauce ingredients. Mix well, and serve with chicken strips for dipping.

MAKES 2 SERVINGS

fried chicken drumsticks with caribbean slaw

Slaw

1 tablespoon light mayonnaise
1 teaspoon seasoned rice vinegar
3 cups bagged coleslaw mix
½ cup pineapple tidbits in juice, lightly drained
¼ cup canned black beans, drained and rinsed
1 teaspoon lime juice
2 tablespoons chopped fresh cilantro

Chicken

¼ cup low-fat buttermilk
½ tablespoon Frank's RedHot Original Cayenne Pepper Sauce
4 raw chicken drumsticks, skin removed
½ cup panko bread crumbs
¾ teaspoon garlic powder
¾ teaspoon onion powder
¼ teaspoon black pepper
¼ teaspoon ground thyme
1 dash salt
¼ cup (about 4 large) egg whites or fat-free egg substitute

398 calories

Prep: 10 minutes

Cook: 20 minutes

Marinate: 1 hour

You'll Need: medium bowl, sealable container, 2 wide mouth bowls, air fryer, nonstick spray

½ of recipe (2 drumsticks with about 1 cup slaw):
398 calories
9g total fat
(2g sat. fat)
828mg sodium
33g carbs
4.5g fiber
13g sugars
45g protein

1. In a medium bowl, thoroughly mix mayo and vinegar. Add coleslaw mix, and stir to coat. Add remaining slaw ingredients. Mix well. Refrigerate until ready to serve.

2. In a sealable container, mix buttermilk with hot sauce. Add drumsticks, and flip to coat. Seal and marinate in the refrigerator for 1 hour.

3. In a wide bowl, mix bread crumbs with seasonings. Place egg whites/substitute in a second wide bowl. Coat drumsticks with egg, followed by the seasoned bread crumbs.

4. Spray an air fryer with nonstick spray. Place drumsticks in the air fryer, and spray with nonstick spray.

5. Set air fryer to 380°F. Cook until crispy and cooked through, 16–18 minutes.

MAKES 2 SERVINGS

french onion chicken tenders with watermelon feta salad

Chicken

⅓ cup panko bread crumbs
1 tablespoon onion soup/dip seasoning mix
¼ cup (about 2 large) egg whites or fat-free liquid egg substitute
10 ounces raw boneless skinless chicken breast, cut into 10 strips

Salad

4 cups baby arugula
2 cups chopped seedless (or seeded) watermelon
1 cup cherry tomatoes, halved
3 tablespoons crumbled feta cheese
1 tablespoon lemon juice

1. In a wide bowl, combine bread crumbs and seasoning mix. Mix well. Place egg whites/substitute in a second wide bowl. Coat chicken with egg, followed by seasoned bread crumbs.

2. Spray an air fryer with nonstick spray. Place chicken in the air fryer.

3. Set air fryer to 360°F. Cook until crispy and cooked through, about 12 minutes.

4. In a large bowl, combine salad ingredients. Lightly toss to mix.

5. Serve chicken alongside or over the salad.

MAKES 2 SERVINGS

---

334 calories

 30m

Prep: 10 minutes

Cook: 15 minutes

You'll Need: 2 wide bowls, air fryer, nonstick spray, large bowl

½ of recipe (5 tenders with about 2½ cups salad):
334 calories
6.5g total fat
(2.5g sat. fat)
550mg sodium
26.5g carbs
2.5g fiber
13g sugars
40.5g protein

crispy lemon garlic chicken

1 lemon, divided
¼ cup panko bread crumbs
2 tablespoons grated Parmesan cheese
½ teaspoon garlic powder
⅛ teaspoon lemon pepper seasoning
⅛ teaspoon salt
¼ cup (about 2 large) egg whites or fat-free liquid egg substitute
Two 5-ounce raw boneless skinless chicken breast cutlets

1. Zest 1 teaspoon of the lemon peel into a wide bowl. Add bread crumbs, Parm, and seasonings. Mix well.

2. Slice lemon in half, and squeeze the juice into a second wide bowl. Add egg whites/substitute, and mix well. Coat chicken with egg mixture, followed by the seasoned bread crumbs.

3. Spray an air fryer with nonstick spray. Place chicken cutlets in the air fryer, and spray with nonstick spray.

4. Set air fryer to 370°F. Cook until crispy and cooked through, about 18 minutes.

MAKES 2 SERVINGS

252 calories

30m

Prep: 10 minutes

Cook: 20 minutes

You'll Need: zester, 2 wide bowls, air fryer, nonstick spray

**½ of recipe
(1 cutlet):**
252 calories
6.5g total fat
(2g sat. fat)
522mg sodium
7.5g carbs
<0.5g fiber
1g sugars
38g protein

elote-topped crispy chicken

Pictured on page 275

¼ cup panko bread crumbs

1 teaspoon taco seasoning, divided

¼ cup (about 2 large) egg whites or fat-free liquid egg substitute

Two 5-ounce raw boneless skinless chicken breast cutlets, pounded to
¼-inch thickness

⅛ teaspoon salt

⅛ teaspoon black pepper

¼ cup frozen sweet corn kernels

2 tablespoons whipped cream cheese

2 tablespoons crumbled feta cheese

⅛ teaspoon cayenne pepper, or more to taste

2 tablespoons chopped fresh cilantro, or more for topping

1. In a wide bowl, mix bread crumbs with ½ teaspoon taco seasoning. Place egg whites/substitute in a second wide bowl.

2. Season chicken with salt and pepper. Coat chicken with egg whites/substitute, followed by the seasoned bread crumbs.

3. Spray an air fryer with nonstick spray. Place chicken in the air fryer, and spray with nonstick spray.

4. Set air fryer to 370°F. Cook until crispy and cooked through, about 18 minutes.

5. In a microwave-safe bowl, combine corn, cream cheese, feta, cayenne pepper, and remaining ½ teaspoon taco seasoning. Mix thoroughly. Microwave for 30 seconds, or until warm.

6. Serve chicken topped with corn mixture and cilantro.

MAKES 2 SERVINGS

pork chops with cabbage & apples

Pictured on page 288

2 cups shredded cabbage
½ cup sliced apple
½ cup sliced onion
1 tablespoon Dijon mustard
1 tablespoon apple cider vinegar
¼ teaspoon salt, divided
¼ teaspoon black pepper, divided
Two 5-ounce boneless pork chops, trimmed of excess fat
¼ teaspoon garlic powder
⅛ teaspoon ground thyme

1. In a medium bowl, combine cabbage, apple, onion, mustard, vinegar, ⅛ teaspoon salt, and ⅛ teaspoon pepper. Mix well.

2. Spray an air fryer with nonstick spray. Season pork chops with garlic powder, thyme, remaining ⅛ teaspoon salt, and remaining ⅛ teaspoon pepper. Place them on one side of the air fryer.

3. Set air fryer to 390°F. Cook pork for 8 minutes.

4. Flip pork. Add cabbage mixture to the other side of the air fryer. Cook until pork is cooked through and cabbage has lightly browned, about 8 more minutes.

MAKES 2 SERVINGS

270 calories

30m

Prep: 10 minutes

Cook: 20 minutes

You'll Need: medium bowl, air fryer, nonstick spray

**½ of recipe
(1 pork chop with
about 1 cup cabbage
& apples):**
270 calories
10g total fat
(3.5g sat. fat)
500mg sodium
10.5g carbs
2.5g fiber
6g sugars
31.5g protein

Pretzel-Coated Pork Tenderloin, opposite page

Pork Chops with Cabbage & Apples, page 287

pretzel-coated pork tenderloin

Pictured on opposite page

1 pound raw pork tenderloin, trimmed of excess fat
1 cup pretzel sticks, finely crushed
3 tablespoons whole wheat flour
¼ teaspoon salt
½ cup (about 4 large) egg whites or fat-free liquid egg substitute
1 tablespoon Dijon mustard
Optional dip: honey mustard

1. Cut pork tenderloin in half horizontally. Cut each piece in half, for a total of four pieces.

2. In a wide bowl, combine crushed pretzels, flour, and salt. Mix well. In a second wide bowl, mix egg whites/substitute with mustard. Coat pork with egg mixture, followed by the pretzel mixture.

3. Spray an air fryer with nonstick spray. Place pork in the air fryer.

4. Set air fryer to 400°F. Cook until cooked through and crispy, 14–16 minutes.

MAKES 4 SERVINGS

207 calories

 5i **30m**

Prep: 10 minutes

Cook: 15 minutes

You'll Need: 2 wide bowls, air fryer, nonstick spray

¼ of recipe:
207 calories
3g total fat
(0.5g sat. fat)
490mg sodium
13.5g carbs
1g fiber
0.5g sugars
29g protein

pistachio-crusted mahi mahi

¼ cup panko bread crumbs

½ ounce (about 2 tablespoons) finely chopped pistachios

½ teaspoon garlic powder

½ teaspoon onion powder

⅛ teaspoon salt

⅛ teaspoon black pepper

2 tablespoons honey mustard

Two 5-ounce raw skinless mahi-mahi fillets

1. In a wide bowl, combine bread crumbs, pistachios, and seasonings. Mix well. Place mustard in a second wide bowl. Coat fish with mustard, followed by bread crumb mixture.

2. Spray an air fryer with nonstick spray. Place fish fillets in the air fryer, and spray with nonstick spray.

3. Set air fryer to 370°F. Cook until crispy and cooked through, 8–10 minutes.

MAKES 2 SERVINGS

218 calories

 5i 30m

Prep: 10 minutes

Cook: 10 minutes

You'll Need: 2 wide bowls, air fryer, nonstick spray

½ of recipe (1 fillet):
218 calories
4g total fat
(0.5g sat. fat)
433mg sodium
13g carbs
1g fiber
5g sugars
28g protein

chili-soy marinated steak with arugula salad

Steak

3 tablespoons sweet chili sauce
1 tablespoon reduced-sodium soy sauce
2 teaspoons sesame seeds
1 teaspoon chopped garlic
Two 4-ounce raw flank steak filets

Salad

1½ tablespoons balsamic vinegar
2 teaspoons olive oil
1 teaspoon Dijon mustard
1 teaspoon honey
1 dash garlic powder
3 cups arugula
½ cup cherry tomatoes, halved

1. In a sealable container, combine chili sauce, soy sauce, sesame seeds, garlic, and 2 teaspoons water. Mix until uniform. Add steak, and flip to coat. Seal and marinate in the refrigerator for 1 hour.

2. Meanwhile, make the salad. In a small bowl, combine vinegar, oil, mustard, honey, and garlic powder. Whisk thoroughly. Place arugula and tomatoes in a large bowl. Add dressing, and toss to coat.

3. Spray an air fryer with nonstick spray. Place steak in the air fryer, and discard excess marinade.

4. Set air fryer to 400°F. Cook to your preference, about 10 minutes for medium-rare.

5. Let steak rest for 5 minutes before slicing.

MAKES 2 SERVINGS

327 calories

Prep: 10 minutes

Cook: 15 minutes

Marinate: 1 hour

You'll Need: sealable container, small bowl, whisk, large bowl, air fryer, nonstick spray

**½ of recipe
(1 filet with about
1½ cups salad):**
327 calories
13.5g total fat
(3.5g sat. fat)
753mg sodium
23.5g carbs
1.5g fiber
18.5g sugars
27g protein

creamy dill salmon

Two 5-ounce raw skinless salmon fillets
⅛ teaspoon plus 1 dash salt, divided
⅛ teaspoon plus 1 dash black pepper, divided
2 tablespoons fat-free plain yogurt, divided
¼ cup panko bread crumbs
⅛ teaspoon garlic powder
⅛ teaspoon onion powder
1 tablespoon creamy mild Dijon mustard
1 teaspoon chopped fresh dill
Serving suggestion: rice and/or riced cauliflower

1. Season salmon with ⅛ teaspoon salt and ⅛ teaspoon pepper.

2. Spray an air fryer with nonstick spray. Place salmon in the air fryer, and spread ½ tablespoon yogurt over each fillet.

3. In a small bowl, combine bread crumbs, garlic powder, onion powder, remaining dash salt, and remaining dash pepper. Mix well. Top salmon with seasoned crumbs.

4. Spray an air fryer with nonstick spray. Place salmon fillets in the air fryer, and spray with nonstick spray.

5. Set air fryer to 400°F. Cook until crispy and cooked through, 10–12 minutes.

6. In a second small bowl, combine remaining 1 tablespoon yogurt with mustard and dill. Stir until smooth and uniform.

7. Serve salmon topped with sauce.

MAKES 2 SERVINGS

273 calories

Prep: 10 minutes

Cook: 15 minutes

You'll Need: air fryer, nonstick spray, 2 small bowls

**½ of recipe
(1 fillet):**
273 calories
11.5g total fat
(3g sat. fat)
506mg sodium
7.5g carbs
0.5g fiber
1.5g sugars
31g protein

fajita stuffed peppers

4 large green bell peppers (look for ones that sit flat)
8 ounces raw extra-lean ground chicken (at least 98% lean)
2 cups frozen riced cauliflower, thawed and drained
½ cup chopped onion
2 teaspoons fajita seasoning
½ cup shredded reduced-fat Mexican-blend cheese
¼ cup fat-free plain Greek yogurt
¼ cup salsa

1. Slice off and discard stem ends of the peppers. Remove and discard seeds.

2. In a medium bowl, combine chicken, cauliflower, onion, and seasoning. Mix thoroughly. Evenly distribute chicken mixture among the peppers.

3. Spray an air fryer with nonstick spray. Place peppers in the air fryer.

4. Set air fryer to 360°F. Cook until peppers are tender and chicken is cooked through, 10–12 minutes.

5. Top with cheese. Cook until melted, about 1 minute.

6. Serve peppers topped with yogurt and salsa.

MAKES 4 SERVINGS

183 calories

Prep: 10 minutes

Cook: 15 minutes

You'll Need: medium bowl, air fryer, nonstick spray

¼ of recipe
(1 stuffed pepper):
183 calories
4g total fat
(2g sat. fat)
355mg sodium
15.5g carbs
4.5g fiber
7.5g sugars
21g protein

HG Heads Up
Not all fajita seasonings are gluten free, so read labels carefully if that's a concern.

fish & chips

Chips

12 ounces (about 1 medium) russet potatoes, peeled and cut in fry-shaped spears
⅛ teaspoon salt

Fish

⅓ cup panko bread crumbs
½ teaspoon chili powder
½ teaspoon garlic powder
⅛ teaspoon salt
⅛ teaspoon black pepper
¼ cup (about 2 large) egg whites or fat-free liquid egg substitute
Two 5-ounce raw cod fillets

Dip

2 tablespoons light mayonnaise
1 tablespoon whipped cream cheese
1 tablespoon fat-free plain Greek yogurt
1 tablespoon chopped pickles
¼ teaspoon dried dill
1 dash garlic powder

368 calories

Prep: 10 minutes

Cook: 25 minutes

You'll Need: air fryer, nonstick spray, 2 wide bowls, small bowl

½ of recipe (1 fillet with about ¾ cups chips):
368 calories
6.5g total fat
(1.5g sat. fat)
662mg sodium
42g carbs
3g fiber
2.5g sugars
34g protein

1. Spray an air fryer with nonstick spray. Place potato spears in the air fryer, and spray with nonstick spray. Season with salt.

2. Set air fryer to 390°F. Cook until crispy, about 15 minutes.

3. Transfer fries to a plate, and cover to keep warm.

4. Meanwhile, prepare the fish. In a wide bowl, mix bread crumbs with seasonings. Place egg whites/substitute in a second wide bowl. Coat fish with egg, followed by the seasoned bread crumbs.

5. Respray the air fryer with nonstick spray. Place fish fillets in the air fryer, and spray with nonstick spray.

6. Set air fryer to 380°F. Cook until crispy and cooked through, 8–10 minutes.

7. In a small bowl, mix dip ingredients.

MAKES 2 SERVINGS

crispy fish tacos

1 tablespoon lime juice
1 teaspoon honey
¼ teaspoon plus 1 dash of salt, divided
⅛ teaspoon plus 1 dash of black pepper, divided
¾ cup bagged coleslaw mix
2 tablespoons chopped fresh cilantro
1 tablespoon seeded and chopped jalapeño pepper
¼ cup panko bread crumbs
½ teaspoon garlic powder
½ teaspoon onion powder
2 tablespoons (about 1 large) egg white or fat-free liquid egg substitute
8 ounces raw cod, cut into 4 pieces
Four 6-inch corn tortillas
2 ounces (about ½ medium) sliced avocado
Optional toppings: salsa, light sour cream

1. In a medium bowl, combine lime juice, honey, 1 dash salt, and 1 dash black pepper. Mix until uniform. Add coleslaw mix, cilantro, and jalapeño pepper. Toss to coat. Refrigerate until ready to serve.

2. In a wide bowl, combine bread crumbs, garlic powder, onion powder, remaining ¼ teaspoon salt, and remaining ⅛ teaspoon black pepper. Mix well.

3. Place egg whites/substitute in a second wide bowl. Coat fish with the egg, followed by the seasoned bread crumbs.

4. Spray an air fryer with nonstick spray. Place fish in the air fryer, and top with any remaining bread crumbs.

5. Set air fryer to 380°F. Cook for 8–10 minutes, until cooked through.

6. Place tortillas between 2 paper towels, and microwave for 15 seconds, or until warm.

7. Top tortillas with slaw, fish, and avocado.

MAKES 2 SERVINGS

303 calories

 30m

Prep: 10 minutes

Cook: 10 minutes

You'll Need: medium bowl, 2 wide bowls, air fryer, nonstick spray

**½ of recipe
(2 tacos):**
303 calories
6.5g total fat
(0.5g sat. fat)
489mg sodium
35g carbs
5.5g fiber
6g sugars
26g protein

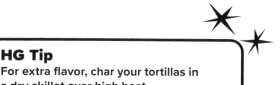

HG Tip
For extra flavor, char your tortillas in a dry skillet over high heat.

tuna croquettes
with apple-cranberry slaw

Slaw

1 tablespoon light mayonnaise
1 tablespoon light balsamic vinaigrette
1 teaspoon Dijon mustard
½ packet natural no-calorie sweetener
3 cups bagged broccoli slaw
⅓ cup chopped Fuji apple
2 tablespoons sweetened dried cranberries, chopped
½ ounce (about 2 tablespoons) sliced almonds

Croquettes

⅔ cup panko bread crumbs, divided
One 5-ounce can albacore tuna packed in water, drained and flaked
⅓ cup (about 4 large) egg whites or fat-free liquid egg substitute
¼ cup finely chopped scallions
2 teaspoons Dijon mustard
1 teaspoon lemon juice
1 teaspoon light mayonnaise
⅛ teaspoon salt
⅛ teaspoon black pepper

351 calories

30m

Prep: 10 minutes

Cook: 15 minutes

You'll Need: 2 medium bowls, air fryer, nonstick spray

½ of recipe (3 croquettes with about 1½ cups slaw):
351 calories
9.5g total fat
(1g sat. fat)
795mg sodium
36.5g carbs
7g fiber
12.5g sugars
27g protein

1. In a medium bowl, combine mayo, vinaigrette, mustard, and sweetener. Mix well. Add remaining slaw ingredients, and toss to coat. Refrigerate until ready to serve.

2. In a second medium bowl, combine ⅓ cup bread crumbs with remaining croquettes ingredients. Mix well.

3. Form tuna mixture into 6 croquettes. Gently coat with remaining bread crumbs.

4. Spray an air fryer with nonstick spray. Place croquettes in the air fryer, and top with any remaining bread crumbs. Spray croquettes with nonstick spray.

5. Set air fryer to 360°F. Cook until lightly browned and crispy, 13–15 minutes.

MAKES 2 SERVINGS

mozzarella-stuffed meatballs with romaine salad

Meatballs

8 ounces raw extra-lean ground beef (at least 95% lean)
¼ cup finely chopped onion
¼ cup panko bread crumbs
3 tablespoons (about 1 large) egg white or fat-free liquid egg substitute
¼ teaspoon Italian seasoning
½ teaspoon garlic powder
⅛ teaspoon salt
⅛ teaspoon black pepper
1 stick light string cheese, sliced into 8 coins
½ cup marinara sauce with 70 calories or less per 2-tablespoon serving

Salad

3 cups chopped romaine lettuce
2 tablespoons finely chopped red onion
⅓ cup sliced cucumber
2 tablespoons sweetened dried cranberries, chopped
2 tablespoons light balsamic vinaigrette

1. In a medium-large bowl, combine all meatball ingredients except string cheese and marinara. Mix thoroughly. Firmly form into 8 meatballs.

2. Press an indentation into each meatball, and fill with a piece of string cheese. Seal meat around cheese.

3. Spray an air fryer with nonstick spray. Place meatballs in the air fryer.

4. Set air fryer to 390°F. Cook for about 10 minutes, until cooked through.

5. Transfer meatballs to a large bowl. Add marinara, and toss to coat.

6. In another large bowl, combine all salad ingredients. Toss to mix.

MAKES 2 SERVINGS

---

326 calories

 30m

Prep: 15 minutes

Cook: 10 minutes

You'll Need: medium-large bowl, air fryer, nonstick spray, 2 large bowls

½ of recipe (4 meatballs with about 1½ cups salad):
326 calories
9g total fat
(3g sat. fat)
719mg sodium
26g carbs
4g fiber
13g sugars
33g protein

sweet chili glazed meatballs with broccoli

Meatballs

8 ounces raw extra-lean ground beef (at least 95% lean)
3 tablespoons (about 1 large) egg white or fat-free liquid egg substitute
¼ cup panko bread crumbs
¼ cup chopped scallions, or more for topping
¼ cup canned water chestnuts, drained and finely chopped
½ teaspoon garlic powder
½ teaspoon ground ginger
2½ cups broccoli florets
2 tablespoons sweet chili sauce
1½ teaspoons reduced-sodium soy sauce
1 teaspoon sesame seeds

1. In a medium-large bowl, combine beef, egg white/substitute, bread crumbs, scallions, water chestnuts, garlic powder, and ginger. Mix thoroughly. Firmly form into 8 meatballs.

2. Spray an air fryer with nonstick spray. Place meatballs in the air fryer.

3. Set air fryer to 390°F. Cook for about 10 minutes, until cooked through.

4. Meanwhile, place broccoli in a microwave-safe bowl with ¼ cup water. Cover and microwave for 3 minutes, or until tender. Drain excess liquid.

5. In a small bowl, combine chili sauce, soy sauce, and 2 teaspoons water. Mix well.

6. Serve meatballs and broccoli topped with chili-soy sauce and sesame seeds.

MAKES 2 SERVINGS

293 calories

30m

Prep: 10 minutes

Cook: 10 minutes

You'll Need: medium-large bowl, air fryer, nonstick spray, microwave-safe bowl, small bowl

½ of recipe (4 meatballs with about 1 cup broccoli):
293 calories
6g total fat
(2g sat. fat)
559mg sodium
27.5g carbs
4g fiber
11g sugars
31g protein

crispy coconut shrimp with green beans

Shrimp

⅓ cup panko bread crumbs
¼ cup unsweetened shredded coconut
1 teaspoon garlic powder
¼ cup (about 2 large) egg whites or fat-free liquid egg substitute
¼ teaspoon coconut extract
8 ounces (about 16) raw large shrimp, peeled, tails removed, deveined

Green Beans

8 ounces green beans, trimmed
1½ teaspoons sesame oil
1 teaspoon chopped garlic
¼ teaspoon salt
⅛ teaspoon black pepper
¼ ounce (about 1 tablespoon) sliced almonds

1. In a wide bowl, combine bread crumbs, shredded coconut, and garlic powder. Mix well.

2. In a second wide bowl, mix egg whites/substitute with coconut extract. Coat shrimp with egg mixture, followed by the bread crumb mixture.

3. Spray an air fryer with nonstick spray. Place shrimp in the air fryer, and spray with nonstick spray.

4. Set air fryer to 390°F. Cook until crispy and cooked through, 10–12 minutes.

5. Meanwhile, prepare the green beans. Bring a large skillet sprayed with nonstick spray to medium heat. Add green beans and 2 tablespoons water. Cover and cook for 8 minutes, or until green beans have mostly softened and water has evaporated. Add oil, garlic, salt, and pepper. Cook and stir until green beans are tender, about 5 minutes. Serve topped with almonds.

MAKES 2 SERVINGS

307 calories

30m

Prep: 10 minutes

Cook: 15 minutes

You'll Need: 2 wide bowls, air fryer, nonstick spray, large skillet with cover

½ of recipe (about 8 shrimp with about ¾ cup green beans):
307 calories
12.5g total fat
(6g sat. fat)
694mg sodium
21g carbs
5g fiber
5g sugars
27g protein

cajun shrimp with corn

1½ tablespoons olive oil
¾ teaspoon garlic powder
½ teaspoon Cajun seasoning
¼ teaspoon paprika
8 ounces (about 16) raw large shrimp, peeled, tails removed, deveined
1 medium ear of corn, husk removed, halved
Optional toppings: lime zest, fresh cilantro

1. In a large bowl, combine oil, garlic powder, Cajun seasoning, and paprika. Mix well. Add shrimp and corn, and toss to coat.

2. Spray an air fryer with nonstick spray. Place shrimp and corn in the air fryer.

3. Set air fryer to 390°F. Cook until shrimp are cooked through and corn has lightly browned, 10–12 minutes.

MAKES 2 SERVINGS

242 calories

Prep: 10 minutes

Cook: 15 minutes

You'll Need: large bowl, air fryer, nonstick spray

½ of recipe
(about 8 shrimp with 1 piece corn):
242 calories
12g total fat
(2g sat. fat)
508mg sodium
11g carbs
1g fiber
3.5g sugars
22.5g protein

sweet chili glazed salmon with blackened corn salad

Salmon

2 tablespoons sweet Asian chili sauce
1½ teaspoons reduced-sodium soy sauce
Two 4-ounce raw skinless salmon fillets
¼ teaspoon garlic powder
2 dashes paprika

Salad

1 cup frozen sweet corn kernels
¼ teaspoon chili powder
¼ teaspoon ground cumin
⅛ teaspoon salt
⅛ teaspoon black pepper
½ cup cherry tomatoes, halved
2 tablespoons chopped fresh cilantro, or more for topping
2 tablespoons finely chopped red onion
1 teaspoon lime juice
⅛ teaspoon salt

1. In a small bowl, mix chili sauce with soy sauce until uniform.

2. Spray an air fryer with nonstick spray. Season salmon with seasonings, and place in the air fryer.

3. Set air fryer to 400°F. Cook for 10–12 minutes, or until cooked through.

4. Meanwhile, make the salad. Bring a skillet sprayed with nonstick spray to medium-high heat. Add corn and seasonings. Cook and stir until blackened, about 5 minutes. Transfer to a large bowl. Add remaining salad ingredients. Mix well.

5. Serve salmon topped with chili-soy sauce and corn salad.

MAKES 2 SERVINGS

309 calories

Prep: 10 minutes

Cook: 15 minutes

You'll Need: small bowl, air fryer, nonstick spray, skillet, large bowl

½ of recipe
(1 fillet with about
¾ cup salad):
309 calories
10g total fat
(2.5g sat. fat)
766mg sodium
28g carbs
2g fiber
13g sugars
26.5g protein

bacon-wrapped scallops

3 slices center-cut bacon or turkey bacon
6 (about 4 ounces) raw large scallops
⅛ teaspoon garlic powder
⅛ teaspoon onion powder

1. Spray an air fryer with nonstick spray. Set air fryer to 400°F. Cook bacon until slightly crispy, about 4 minutes, flipping halfway through.

2. Meanwhile, season scallops with garlic powder and onion powder.

3. Transfer bacon to a cutting board. Cut each piece in half widthwise. Wrap a half slice of bacon around each scallop, and secure with a toothpick.

4. Set air fryer to 400°F. Place bacon-wrapped scallops in the air fryer. Cook until scallops are cooked through and bacon is crispy, 5–7 minutes.

MAKES 1 SERVING

178 calories

Prep: 10 minutes

Cook: 15 minutes

You'll Need: air fryer, nonstick spray

Entire recipe:
178 calories
7.5g total fat
(2.5g sat. fat)
878mg sodium
4.5g carbs
0g fiber
0g sugars
21.5g protein

steak marsala

8 ounces raw lean steak, cut into bite-sized pieces
½ teaspoon garlic powder
¼ teaspoon salt
¼ teaspoon black pepper
3 cups sliced mushrooms
¼ cup marsala wine
1½ teaspoons cornstarch
1 tablespoon whipped butter

1. Season steak with garlic powder, salt, and pepper.

2. Spray an air fryer with nonstick spray. Place steak and mushrooms in the air fryer.

3. Set air fryer to 390°F. Cook until steak is fully cooked and mushrooms are tender, about 8 minutes.

4. Meanwhile, prepare the sauce. In a small microwave-safe bowl, combine wine with cornstarch. Stir to dissolve. (Whisk, if needed.) Add butter. Microwave for 30 seconds, or until hot and thickened. Mix well.

5. Serve steak and mushrooms topped with sauce.

MAKES 2 SERVINGS

273 calories

Prep: 5 minutes

Cook: 10 minutes

You'll Need: air fryer, nonstick spray, small microwave-safe bowl, whisk (optional)

½ of recipe:
273 calories
10.5g total fat
(5g sat. fat)
570mg sodium
11g carbs
1g fiber
6g sugars
28g protein

BBQ tofu bites

½ cup panko bread crumbs
2 teaspoons sesame seeds, or more for topping
1 teaspoon garlic powder, divided
1 teaspoon onion powder, divided
¼ teaspoon plus ⅛ teaspoon salt, divided
¼ teaspoon black pepper, divided
1 pound extra-firm tofu, excess moisture removed, cubed
¼ cup **BBQ sauce**, or more for dipping
Optional topping: fresh cilantro

1. In a wide bowl, combine bread crumbs, sesame seeds, ¾ teaspoon garlic powder, ¾ teaspoon onion powder, ⅛ teaspoon salt, and ⅛ teaspoon pepper. Mix well.

2. In a large bowl, season tofu with remaining ¼ teaspoon garlic powder, ¼ teaspoon onion powder, ¼ teaspoon salt, and ⅛ teaspoon pepper. Add BBQ sauce, and gently toss to coat.

3. Gently coat tofu with seasoned bread crumbs.

4. Spray an air fryer with nonstick spray. Place half of the tofu bites in the air fryer, and spray with nonstick spray.

5. Set air fryer to 370°F. Cook until golden brown and crispy, 10–12 minutes, flipping halfway through.

6. Repeat with remaining tofu bites.

MAKES 4 SERVINGS

190 calories

5i **V**

Prep: 15 minutes

Cook: 25 minutes

You'll Need: wide bowl, large bowl, air fryer, nonstick spray

¼ of recipe
(about ¾ cup):
190 calories
7.5g total fat
(0.5g sat. fat)
398mg sodium
16g carbs
1.5g fiber
6.5g sugars
14g protein

HG Tip
Use paper towels to remove as much moisture as possible from the tofu. It'll crisp up much better this way!

Another HG Tip
Serve these crispy nuggets over veggies, or dip them in something yummy like honey mustard or light ranch!

falafel with yogurt sauce

Falafel

1 cup canned chickpeas (garbanzo beans), drained and rinsed
½ cup very finely chopped onion
¼ cup whole wheat flour
3 tablespoons (about 1 large) egg white or fat-free liquid egg substitute
2 tablespoons finely chopped fresh parsley, or more for topping
1 tablespoon chopped fresh cilantro
1 tablespoon ground cumin
1 tablespoon chopped garlic
¼ teaspoon lemon juice
¼ teaspoon paprika
⅛ teaspoon salt

Sauce

¼ cup fat-free plain Greek yogurt
1 tablespoon crumbled feta cheese
½ teaspoon dried dill
¼ teaspoon garlic powder
⅛ teaspoon lemon juice

1. Place chickpeas in a large bowl, and thoroughly mash with a potato masher. Add remaining falafel ingredients, and mix thoroughly. Firmly and evenly form into eight balls.

2. Spray an air fryer with nonstick spray. Place falafel in the air fryer.

3. Set air fryer to 370°F. Cook until light golden brown, 14–16 minutes.

4. Meanwhile, combine sauce ingredients in a small bowl. Mix until uniform.

5. Serve falafel with sauce.

MAKES 2 SERVINGS

244 calories

Prep: 10 minutes

Cook: 20 minutes

You'll Need: large bowl, potato masher, air fryer, nonstick spray, small bowl

½ of recipe
(4 falafel with about
2 tablespoons sauce):
244 calories
3.5g total fat
(0.5g sat. fat)
446mg sodium
39.5g carbs
9.5g fiber
4.5g sugars
15.5g protein

desserts

strawberry cheesecake egg rolls

Pictured on pages 324–325

½ cup whipped cream cheese
½ cup light/low-fat ricotta cheese
3 packets natural no-calorie sweetener
½ teaspoon vanilla extract
⅛ teaspoon cinnamon
1½ cups chopped freeze-dried strawberries
6 egg roll wrappers
Optional topping: powdered sugar

1. In a medium bowl, combine cream cheese, ricotta, sweetener, vanilla extract, and cinnamon. Mix well. Gently fold in freeze-dried strawberries.

2. Evenly distribute ⅙ of the filling (about ¼ cup) along the center of an egg roll wrapper. Fold in the sides, and roll up the wrapper around the filling. Seal with a dab of water. Repeat to make five more egg rolls.

3. Spray an air fryer with nonstick spray. Place egg rolls in the air fryer, and spray with nonstick spray.

4. Set air fryer to 390°F. Cook until golden brown, about 6 minutes.

MAKES 6 SERVINGS

141 calories

Prep: 10 minutes

Cook: 10 minutes

You'll Need: medium bowl, air fryer, nonstick spray

⅙ of recipe
(1 egg roll):
141 calories
4g total fat
(2.5g sat. fat)
200mg sodium
21.5g carbs
2g fiber
5.5g sugars
4.5g protein

apple pie egg rolls

Pictured on pages 324–325

2 teaspoons cornstarch
3 cups peeled and chopped Fuji or Gala apples
2 packets natural no-calorie sweetener
1 teaspoon cinnamon
¼ teaspoon vanilla extract
⅛ teaspoon salt
6 egg roll wrappers
Optional topping: powdered sugar

1. In a medium nonstick pot, combine cornstarch with ½ cup water. Whisk to dissolve.

2. Add apples, sweetener, cinnamon, vanilla extract, and salt. Stir well.

3. Set heat to medium. Stirring frequently, cook until apples have slightly softened and mixture is thick and gooey, 8–10 minutes.

4. Transfer to a medium bowl. Let cool completely, about 1 hour.

5. Evenly distribute ⅙ of the filling (about ¼ cup) along the center of an egg roll wrapper. Fold in the sides, and roll up the wrapper around the filling. Seal with a dab of water. Repeat to make five more egg rolls.

6. Spray an air fryer with nonstick spray. Place egg rolls in the air fryer, and spray with nonstick spray.

7. Set air fryer to 390°F. Cook until golden brown, about 6 minutes.

MAKES 6 SERVINGS

94 calories

Prep: 10 minutes

Cook: 20 minutes

Cool: 1 hour

You'll Need: nonstick pot, whisk, medium bowl, air fryer, nonstick spray

**⅙ of recipe
(1 egg roll):**
94 calories
0.5g total fat
(0g sat. fat)
162mg sodium
21.5g carbs
1.5g fiber
6g sugars
2g protein

Apple Pie Egg Rolls,
page 323

Sweet
Cinnamon
Churros,
page 327

Strawberry Cheesecake
Egg Rolls, page 322

Tropical
Cheesecake
Bites, page 328

Peach Cobbler Bites
page 326

peach cobbler bites

Pictured on pages 324–325

1 medium peach
¼ cup panko bread crumbs
1 packet natural no-calorie sweetener
¼ teaspoon cinnamon, or more for topping
1 dash salt
¼ cup (about 2 large) egg whites or fat-free liquid egg substitute
¼ teaspoon vanilla extract
Optional dips/toppings: light whipped topping, light vanilla yogurt

1. Remove peach pit, and cut peach into half-moon slices, about ½-inch thick.

2. In a wide bowl, combine bread crumbs, sweetener, cinnamon, and salt. Mix well.

3. In a second wide bowl, mix egg whites/substitute with vanilla extract. Coat peach slices with egg mixture, followed by the seasoned bread crumbs.

4. Spray an air fryer with nonstick spray. Place peach slices in the air fryer, and spray with nonstick spray.

5. Set air fryer to 390°F. Cook until golden brown and crispy, 6–8 minutes.

MAKES 1 SERVING

144 calories

Prep: 10 minutes

Cook: 10 minutes

You'll Need: 2 wide bowls, air fryer, nonstick spray

Entire recipe:
144 calories
0.5g total fat
(0g sat. fat)
253mg sodium
28.5g carbs
3g fiber
14g sugars
6g protein

sweet cinnamon churros

Pictured on pages 324–325

½ cup self-rising flour
3 packets natural no-calorie sweetener, divided
1½ teaspoons cinnamon, divided
⅛ teaspoon salt
½ cup fat-free plain Greek yogurt
1 tablespoon whipped butter, melted

1. In a large bowl, combine flour, 1 sweetener packet, ½ teaspoon cinnamon, and salt. Mix well. Add yogurt, and mix until dough forms.

2. Roll out dough into a square about 6 inches by 6 inches and ¼ inch thick. Cut dough into 6 strips. Gently roll strips into cylinders, and twist each one twice to form a churro.

3. In a small bowl, mix remaining 2 sweetener packets with remaining 1 teaspoon cinnamon.

4. Brush churros with melted butter, and top with cinnamon mixture.

5. Spray an air fryer with nonstick spray. Place churros in the air fryer.

6. Set air fryer to 360°F. Cook until golden brown, about 12 minutes.

MAKES 2 SERVINGS

175 calories

Prep: 10 minutes

Cook: 15 minutes

You'll Need: large bowl, small bowl, air fryer, nonstick spray

**½ of recipe
(3 churros):**
175 calories
3g total fat
(2g sat. fat)
547mg sodium
27g carbs
1g fiber
2g sugars
8.5g protein

tropical cheesecake bites

Pictured on pages 324–325

½ cup pineapple tidbits packed in juice, thoroughly drained and
    roughly chopped
¼ cup whipped cream cheese
1 tablespoon unsweetened shredded coconut
2 teaspoon honey
⅛ teaspoon coconut extract
1 dash cinnamon
8 gyoza or wonton wrappers
Optional dip: light whipped topping

1. In a medium bowl, combine all ingredients except wrappers.
   Mix until uniform.

2. Top a wrapper with ⅛ of the mixture (about 1½ tablespoons).
   Moisten the edges with water, and fold in half, enclosing the
   filling. Press firmly on the edges to seal. Repeat to make seven
   more cheesecake bites.

3. Spray an air fryer with nonstick spray. Place cheesecake bites
   in the air fryer, and spray with nonstick spray.

4. Set air fryer to 370°F. Cook until golden brown and crispy,
   about 4 minutes.

MAKES 4 SERVINGS

99 calories

Prep: 10 minutes

Cook: 5 minutes

You'll Need: medium
bowl, air fryer, nonstick
spray

¼ of recipe
(2 bites):
99 calories
3g total fat
(2g sat. fat)
116mg sodium
16g carbs
<0.5g fiber
7g sugars
1.5g protein

blueberry-lemon chomptarts

Pictured on pages 330–331

¼ **cup frozen blueberries**
¼ **teaspoon cornstarch**
¼ **teaspoon lemon zest, or more for topping**
½ **cup self-rising flour**
½ **cup fat-free vanilla Greek yogurt**
3 **tablespoons natural no-calorie powdered sweetener**
1½ **teaspoons lemon juice**
Optional topping: lemon zest

1. In a small bowl, combine blueberries, cornstarch, and lemon zest. Mix well.

2. In a large bowl, mix flour and yogurt until dough forms.

3. Shape dough into two rectangles, each about 7 inches by 5 inches and ¼ inch thick. Slice each rectangle in half widthwise for a total of four rectangles.

4. Spoon blueberry mixture over two rectangles, leaving ½-inch borders. Top each of these rectangles with one of the remaining rectangles. Firmly press edges with a fork to seal.

5. Spray an air fryer with nonstick spray. Place tarts in the air fryer, and spray with nonstick spray.

6. Set air fryer to 360°F. Cook until light golden brown and cooked through, 10–12 minutes.

7. In a second small bowl, mix sweetener and lemon juice until uniform. Drizzle over tarts.

MAKES 2 SERVINGS

162 calories

Prep: 10 minutes

Cook: 15 minutes

You'll Need: 2 small bowls, large bowl, air fryer, nonstick spray

**½ of recipe
(1 tart):**
162 calories
<0.5g total fat
(0g sat. fat)
377mg sodium
50g carbs
0.5g fiber
8g sugars
7g protein

S'mores Chomptarts,
page 332

Blueberry-Lemon Chomptarts,
page 329

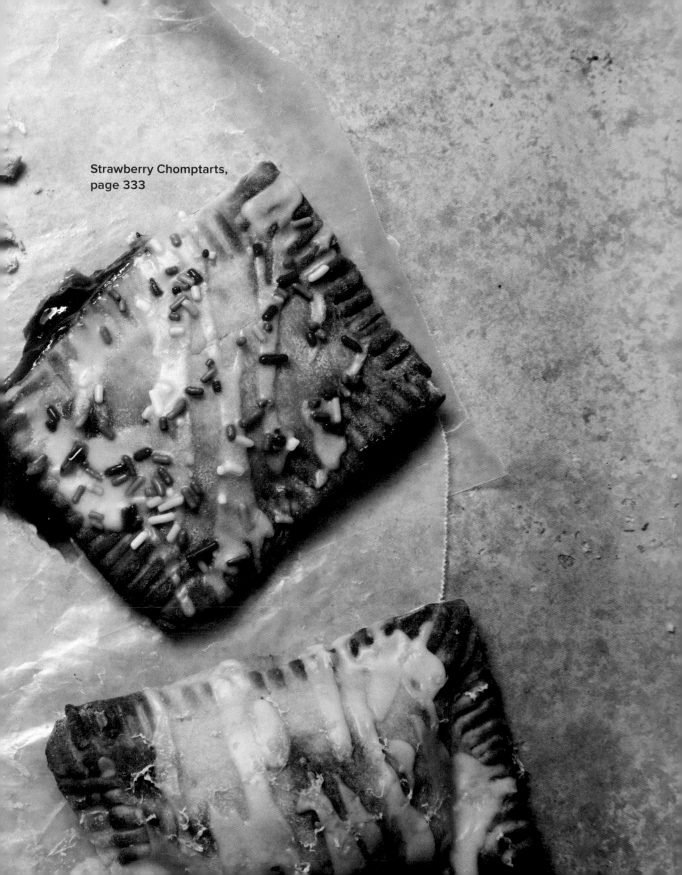

Strawberry Chomptarts,
page 333

s'mores chomptarts

Pictured on pages 330–331

½ cup self-rising flour
½ cup fat-free vanilla Greek yogurt
3 tablespoons mini marshmallows
1 tablespoon mini semi-sweet chocolate chips
3 tablespoons natural no-calorie powdered sweetener
1½ teaspoons unsweetened vanilla almond milk
1 graham cracker (¼ sheet), crushed

1. In a large bowl, mix flour and yogurt until dough forms.

2. Shape dough into two rectangles, about 7 inches by 5 inches wide and ¼ inch thick. Evenly slice each rectangle in half width-wise to make a total of 4 smaller rectangles.

3. Evenly divide marshmallows and chocolate chips over two rectangles, leaving ½-inch borders. Top each of these rectangles with one of the remaining rectangles. Firmly press edges with a fork to seal.

4. Spray an air fryer with nonstick spray. Place chomptarts in the air fryer, and spray with nonstick spray.

5. Set air fryer to 360°F. Cook until light golden brown and cooked through, 10–12 minutes.

6. Meanwhile, in a small bowl, mix sweetener and milk until uniform. Drizzle over chomptarts.

7. Top with crushed graham cracker.

MAKES 2 SERVINGS

208 calories

Prep: 10 minutes

Cook: 15 minutes

You'll Need: large bowl, air fryer, nonstick spray, small bowl

**½ of recipe
(1 tart):**
208 calories
2.5g total fat
(1.5g sat. fat)
410mg sodium
56g carbs
0.5g fiber
13g sugars
7.5g protein

strawberry chomptarts

Pictured on pages 330–331

½ cup self-rising flour
½ cup fat-free vanilla Greek yogurt
3 tablespoons low-sugar strawberry preserves
2½ tablespoons natural no-calorie powdered sweetener
1½ teaspoons unsweetened vanilla almond milk
2 teaspoons rainbow sprinkles

1. In a large bowl, mix flour and yogurt until dough forms.

2. Shape dough into a large rectangle, about 7 inches by 10 inches and ¼ inch thick. Slice in half widthwise and lengthwise for a total of 4 rectangles.

3. Spread preserves onto two rectangles, leaving ½-inch borders. Top each of these rectangles with one of the remaining rectangles. Firmly press edges with a fork to seal.

4. Spray an air fryer with nonstick spray. Place tarts in the air fryer, and spray with nonstick spray.

5. Set air fryer to 360°F. Cook until light golden brown and cooked through, 10–12 minutes.

6. In a small bowl, mix sweetener and milk until sweetener dissolves and mixture is smooth and uniform. Drizzle over tarts. Top with sprinkles.

MAKES 2 SERVINGS

208 calories

Prep: 10 minutes

Cook: 15 minutes

You'll Need: large bowl, air fryer, nonstick spray, small bowl

½ of recipe (1 tart):
208 calories
0.5g total fat
(0g sat. fat)
390mg sodium
56g carbs
0.5g fiber
16g sugars
7g protein

chomptart 101

These tasty treats are made possible thanks to 2-ingredient dough, a Hungry Girl staple! For tips, tricks, and more recipes with the dough, flip to page 187.

Natural no-calorie powdered sweetener is the powdered sugar swap of your dreams. It measures cup-for-cup like regular powdered sugar (a.k.a. confectioners sugar), and it's delicious in desserts like these. Look for it in stores, or buy it on Amazon.

You've reached the end of the book. If you're looking for more recipes, tips & tricks, sign up for my free daily emails at hungry-girl.com. 🍜!!

'Til next time . . . Chew the right thing!

Xo

Lisa

index